How to use your Snap Revi:

CW00358341

This *Romeo and Juliet* Snap Revision Text Guide will
Edexcel English Literature exam. It is divided into tv
easily find help for the bits you find tricky. This boo
to know for the exam:

Plot: what happens in the play?

Setting and Context: what periods, places, events and attitudes are relevant to
understanding the play?

Characters: who are the main characters, how are they presented, and how do
they change?

Themes: what ideas does the author explore in the play, and how are they shown?

The Exam: what kinds of question will come up in your exam, and how can you
get top marks?

To help you get ready for your exam, each two-page topic includes the following:

Key Quotations to Learn
Short quotations to memorise that will allow you to analyse in the exam and boost
your grade.

Summary
A recap of the most important points covered in the topic.

Sample Analysis
An example of the kind of analysis that the examiner will be looking for.

Quick Test
A quick-fire test to check you can remember the main points from the topic.

Exam Practice
A short writing task so you can practise applying what you've covered in the topic.

Glossary
A handy list of words you will find useful when revising *Romeo and Juliet* with
easy-to-understand definitions.

AUTHOR:
IAN
KIRBY

ebook

To access the ebook version of this
Snap Revision Text Guide, visit
collins.co.uk/ebooks
and follow the step-by-step instructions.

Published by Collins
An imprint of HarperCollins*Publishers*
1 London Bridge Street
London SE1 9GF

HarperCollins*Publishers*
1st Floor, Watermarque Building,
Ringsend Road,
Dublin 4, Ireland

MIX
Paper from
responsible source

FSC
www.fsc.org FSC™ C007454

This book is produced from independently
certified FSC™ paper to ensure responsible
forest management.

For more information visit:
www.harpercollins.co.uk/green

© HarperCollins*Publishers* Limited 2019

ISBN 978-0-00-835304-9

First published 2019
This edition published 2022

10 9 8 7 6 5 4 3 2

All rights reserved. No part of this publication
may be reproduced, stored in a retrieval
system, or transmitted, in any form or by any
means, electronic, mechanical, photocopying,
recording or otherwise, without the prior
permission of Collins.

British Library Cataloguing in Publication Data.

A CIP record of this book is available from the
British Library.

Commissioning editor: Fiona McGlade
Project management: Shelley Teasdale and
Richard Toms
Author: Ian Kirby
Proofreader: Tracey Cowell
Typesetting: Mark Steward and QBS Learning
Cover designers: Kneath Associates and
    Sarah Duxbury
Production: Karen Nulty
Printed and bound in the UK using 100%
Renewable Electricity at CPI Group (UK) Ltd

ACKNOWLEDGEMENTS
The author and publisher are grateful to
the copyright holders for permission to use
quoted materials and images.
Every effort has been made to trace copyright
holders and obtain their permission for the
use of copyright material. The author and
publisher will gladly receive information
enabling them to rectify any error or omission
in subsequent editions. All facts are correct at
time of going to press.

Contents

The Prologue and Act 1 scenes 1 and 2

You must be able to: understand what happens in the first half of Act 1.

The Prologue

The play begins with a **sonnet**, which summarises the events of the play. The audience is told of two wealthy families at war, 'Two households both alike in dignity', and two young people falling in love and eventually killing themselves, 'A pair of star-cross'd lovers take their life'.

Shakespeare does this to increase the sense of **fate**: all the time that the audience is watching Romeo and Juliet's romance unfold, there is a growing sense of **tragedy**.

Act 1 scene 1

Using lots of witty **wordplay**, two Capulet servants, Gregory and Sampson, discuss the family feud with the Montagues. Abraham and Balthasar, two Montague servants, arrive and Sampson decides to be insulting, 'I will bite my thumb at them'.

A swordfight begins but is broken up by the appearance of Benvolio, a Montague. However, his entrance is quickly followed by Tybalt, a Capulet, who is more aggressive, 'Have at thee, coward'.

The fight resumes and develops further when Lord Montague and Lord Capulet arrive (despite their wives trying to stop them). Prince Escalus stops the fighting and announces that if there is another disturbance, the penalty will be death.

The characters leave the stage, apart from Benvolio and Lord and Lady Montague. They discuss Romeo who is presented as a solitary and **melancholy** young man. Lord Montague asks Benvolio to help find out the reason for Romeo's unhappiness. As Romeo appears on stage, his parents leave and Benvolio cheerfully approaches his cousin.

Romeo is suffering from **unrequited love**, 'From love's weak childish bow she lives uncharm'd'. The audience later discover that the girl's name is Rosaline. Romeo's speech is full of **oxymorons**, 'Feather of lead, bright smoke, cold fire, sick health', to show his inner turmoil.

Act 1 scene 2

Lord Capulet discusses Prince Escalus's orders with Paris, a wealthy young nobleman.

Paris wishes to marry Capulet's daughter, Juliet, but Capulet wants him to wait 'two more summers' as he thinks Juliet is too young for a successful marriage.

He describes his love for his only child and encourages Paris to 'get her heart', adding that his daughter's decision is important, 'my will to her consent is but a part'. Capulet invites Paris to the evening's feast.

As they leave, a servant is delivering invitations. He meets Romeo and Benvolio, who discover that Rosaline will be at the feast. Benvolio convinces Romeo to attend, hoping that his cousin will fall in love with someone else.

Key Quotations to Learn

Sampson: 'when I have fought with the men I will be civil with the maids, I will cut off their heads. [...] or their maidenheads,' (Ii)

Tybalt: 'What, drawn, and talk of peace? I hate the word, / As I hate hell, all Montagues, and thee:' (Ii)

Lord Montague: 'Thou villain Capulet! Hold me not! Let me go!'
Lady Montague: 'Thou shalt not stir one foot to seek a foe.' (Ii)

Summary

- The start of the play introduces the feud between the Montagues and the Capulets.
- Romeo is presented as a romantic and melancholy young man.
- Lord Capulet reveals his love and care for his daughter, Juliet.
- Paris is introduced as a suitor for Juliet's love.

Questions

QUICK TEST
1. Who starts the fight between the Montagues and the Capulets in Act 1 scene 1?
2. How do Benvolio and Tybalt's attitudes to the fight differ?
3. Why does Lord Capulet want Paris to wait for two years before marrying Juliet?
4. Why does Romeo want to attend the Capulet feast and why does Benvolio want him to attend?

EXAM PRACTICE
Using one or more of the 'Key Quotations to Learn', write a paragraph analysing how the feud between the Montagues and the Capulets is presented in the opening scenes of Act 1.

Act 1 scenes 3 to 5

You must be able to: understand what happens in the second half of Act 1.

Act 1 scene 3

Lady Capulet and the Nurse talk about Juliet's age. The Nurse is very talkative and makes rude jokes.

In contrast to her husband, Lady Capulet thinks her daughter should be married by now. Juliet says she has not thought about marriage yet, but her mother is insistent. She and the Nurse praise Paris; Lady Capulet uses lots of romantic images (such as 'precious book of love'), while the Nurse makes a joke about pregnancy ('Women grow by men'). Juliet agrees to consider Paris.

Act 1 scene 4

Romeo and Benvolio arrive with Mercutio at the Capulets' feast. It is a **masquerade** so the two Montagues aren't recognised.

Romeo is still feeling melancholy so Mercutio encourages him to dance. They talk about love and Mercutio makes rude sexual **innuendos**. Romeo begins to talk about a dream that he has had but, instead, Mercutio tells the story of a fairy called Queen Mab and her power over dreamers.

Act 1 scene 5

Lord Capulet cheerfully welcomes his guests to the feast.

Romeo spots Juliet dancing and asks one of the servants who she is but, because it is a masquerade, he does not know. Romeo is struck by Juliet's beauty, comparing her to a 'rich jewel' and a 'snowy dove'. He forgets Rosaline and decides that he is now properly in love, 'For I ne'er saw true beauty till this night'.

Tybalt recognises Romeo's voice but is stopped from fighting by Lord Capulet. He tells him to calm down and describes Romeo as behaving 'like a portly gentleman'. He comments on how everyone considers Romeo to be 'a virtuous and well-govern'd youth'.

After Tybalt refuses to ignore Romeo, Lord Capulet loses his temper, shouts at Tybalt and insults him, reminding him that he is the master of the house and that he will be obeyed. Tybalt does as he is told but says he will bear a bitter grudge against Romeo.

Unaware of the scene he has caused, Romeo approaches Juliet. Their first dialogue together is written in the form of a sonnet that ends with them kissing. It is love at first sight but Juliet is called away to her mother.

Romeo realises that Juliet is a Capulet, 'Is she a Capulet? / O dear account. My life is my foe's debt'.

Juliet discovers that Romeo is a Montague, 'My only love sprung from my only hate'.

Key Quotations to Learn

Lady Capulet: 'Well think of marriage now.' (Iiii)

Romeo: 'O, she doth teach the torches to burn bright!' (Iv)

Juliet: 'Go ask his name. If he be married, / My grave is like to be my wedding bed.' (Iv)

Summary

- Unlike her husband, Lady Capulet thinks Juliet should get married and encourages her to marry Paris.
- Romeo and Benvolio go to the Capulet feast with Mercutio.
- Tybalt is angry when he realises Romeo is at the party. Tybalt argues with Lord Capulet, who doesn't want any fighting, and Tybalt's resentment towards Romeo grows.
- Romeo and Juliet fall in love at first sight. They talk and kiss before discovering that they come from rival families.

Questions

QUICK TEST
1. How do Lady Capulet and the Nurse talk differently about love?
2. Why aren't Romeo and Benvolio recognised as Montagues at the feast?
3. What happens to Romeo's love for Rosaline?
4. Why does Lord Capulet lose his temper with Tybalt?
5. What form of poetry does Shakespeare use when writing Romeo and Juliet's first piece of dialogue together? Why?

EXAM PRACTICE
Using one or more of the 'Key Quotations to Learn', write a paragraph analysing how love and/or marriage is presented in the second half of Act 1.

Act 2 scenes 1 to 3

You must be able to: understand what happens in the first half of Act 2.

Act 2 scene 1

The second act begins with Romeo not wanting to leave Juliet. As Benvolio and Mercutio come looking for him, he hides.

Mercutio jokingly pretends he will 'conjure' Romeo to reappear, mocking their friend's romantic nature and using lots of sexual innuendos about his desire for Rosaline ('in his mistress' name / I conjure only but to raise him up'). They decide that Romeo wants to be alone and they leave.

Act 2 scene 2

Romeo emerges from his hiding place and stands beneath the balcony of Juliet's bedroom. Throughout the scene, romantic images are **juxtaposed** with references to death or pain, such as 'Arise fair sun and kill the envious moon', to remind the audience that Romeo and Juliet's love is doomed.

Romeo watches Juliet and compares her to the sun, stars and an angel. Juliet's speech focuses on the obstacle of Romeo being a Montague. Romeo says to himself that he will give up his name and 'be new baptis'd' for her.

Juliet overhears him and they begin to talk. She is worried that he will be caught by her family and killed. He describes the power of his love and says he is not scared but would rather be dead if she does not love him.

She is embarrassed that he has overheard her talking about him and asks him if he truly loves her, 'If thou dost love, pronounce it faithfully'. He begins to swear his love but she begins to worry that they are rushing things ('It is too rash, too unadvis'd, too sudden'). She hopes that when they next meet, their 'bud of love' will have grown into 'a beauteous flower'.

They are interrupted by the Nurse calling to Juliet. They proclaim their love for each other and Juliet suggests they marry the next day.

Act 2 scene 3

Friar Laurence is tending his plants and describing their medicinal properties. His speech is full of images of life and death.

Romeo arrives and the Friar is friendly, joking that he can tell Romeo hasn't been to bed and asking if he was with Rosaline.

He explains that he has fallen in love with a Capulet and asks the Friar to join them in marriage later that day. The Friar worries about how quickly Romeo has forgotten Rosaline but he agrees to the ceremony, hoping that 'this alliance may so happy prove / To turn your households' rancour to pure love'.

Key Quotations to Learn

Juliet: 'What's in a name? That which we call a rose / By any other name would smell as sweet;' (IIii)

Romeo: 'My name, dear saint, is hateful to myself / Because it is an enemy to thee.' (IIii)

Romeo: 'Alack, there lies more peril in thine eye / Than twenty of their swords.' (IIii)

Summary

- Rather than leave the Capulet feast with Benvolio and Mercutio, Romeo watches Juliet on her balcony.
- He describes how beautiful she is, as she expresses her wish that he wasn't a Montague.
- They confess their love for each other and arrange to marry the next day.
- Friar Laurence agrees to perform the marriage, hoping that it will bring the two feuding families together.

Questions

QUICK TEST
1. Why does Shakespeare include references to death in his descriptions of romance?
2. Why does Juliet appear to want to take her relationship with Romeo slowly?
3. Where does she speed up the relationship?
4. What reservation does Friar Laurence have about Romeo's love for Juliet?

EXAM PRACTICE
Using one or more of the 'Key Quotations to Learn', write a paragraph analysing how love is presented as problematic in Act 2 scene 2.

You must be able to: understand what happens in the second half of Act 2.

Act 2 scene 4

Benvolio and Mercutio discuss Romeo, still believing he is suffering from unrequited love for Rosaline. It is also revealed that Tybalt has written to Romeo, challenging him for his presence at the Capulet feast. Mercutio admits that Tybalt is a good fighter but also ridicules him.

Romeo appears and is more cheerful than at the start of the play, showing the positive effect of his love for Juliet. He trades **puns** and sexual innuendos with Mercutio who adds, 'Why is not this better now than groaning for love? Now art thou sociable, now art thou Romeo'. However, Romeo keeps his relationship with Juliet secret.

The Nurse enters the stage, along with her servant, Peter. Before Mercutio and Benvolio leave, Mercutio makes fun of the Nurse, calling her ugly ('hide her face'), suggesting she is a prostitute ('A bawd!') and using **irony** to suggest her lack of class ('farewell lady, lady, lady').

The Nurse warns Romeo that if he is not being true and faithful to Juliet then his behaviour is contemptible. He reassures her and passes on the message that Juliet should go to Friar Laurence in the afternoon, where they will meet and be married.

Act 2 scene 5

Juliet waits anxiously for the Nurse to return with news of Romeo, 'O God she comes. O honey Nurse, what news? / Hast thou met with him?'

Instead of giving her news straight away, the Nurse talks about her aching bones, her lack of breath, her headache and her back pain.

Juliet flatteringly encourages her to get to the point, 'Sweet, sweet, sweet Nurse, tell me, what says my love?', but also gets annoyed, 'How art thou out of breath when thou hast breath / To say to me thou art out of breath?'

Eventually, to Juliet's relief and happiness, the Nurse reveals the marriage plan for the afternoon.

Act 2 scene 6

Friar Laurence talks to Romeo and still has mixed feelings about the marriage; he is both hopeful and worried about the outcome of a Montague marrying a Capulet.

He advises caution and taking their time, which is immediately contrasted with Juliet's arrival on stage: *Enter Juliet somewhat fast and embraces Romeo*.

As with previous scenes, references to love are juxtaposed with references to death in order to explore the idea that their love is doomed.

The act ends with the Friar leading Romeo and Juliet to the wedding ceremony.

Key Quotations to Learn

Juliet: 'Love's heralds should be thoughts / Which ten times faster glide than the sun's beams,' (IIv)

Romeo: 'Then love-devouring death do what he dare: / It is enough I may but call her mine.' (IIvi)

Friar Laurence: 'Therefore love moderately; long love doth so. / Too swift arrives as tardy as too slow.' (IIvi)

Summary

- Romeo is happy about his forthcoming marriage to Juliet but doesn't confide in his friends.
- He sends word about the wedding to Juliet via the Nurse.
- Juliet waits anxiously for news and the Nurse annoys her by not getting straight to the point.
- Despite Friar Laurence's reservations, he prepares to marry Romeo and Juliet.

Questions

QUICK TEST
1. What change in Romeo does Mercutio notice?
2. When is the wedding arranged to take place?
3. Why is Juliet anxious for the Nurse's return?
4. Which characters warn Romeo about aspects of his relationship with Juliet?

EXAM PRACTICE
Using one or more of the 'Key Quotations to Learn', write a paragraph analysing how feelings about love are presented in the second half of Act 2.

Act 3 scenes 1 and 2

You must be able to: understand what happens in the first half of Act 3.

Act 3 scene 1

Benvolio and Mercutio are on the streets of Verona with a group of Montagues. Benvolio wants to go home to avoid the possibility of meeting any Capulets and a fight breaking out. However, Mercutio ridicules Benvolio for talking about peace but having a violent, quarrelsome temper.

When Tybalt appears with other Capulets, Benvolio is worried but Mercutio does not care. Tybalt and Mercutio begin to argue.

Tybalt changes his attention to Romeo when he arrives on stage. He calls him a villain but Romeo tries to avoid the argument. Although he doesn't reveal his marriage to Juliet, he says, 'good Capulet, which name I tender / As dearly as my own'.

Mercutio is angered by Romeo's 'calm, dishonourable, vile submission' and decides to fight Tybalt himself.

They draw their swords and begin to fight. Romeo tries to stop them, asking Benvolio to help him. While Romeo holds him back, Mercutio is stabbed by Tybalt who then exits the stage.

Mercutio curses the Montagues and the Capulets but jokes about his wound even though it is fatal.

Romeo realises that he is the indirect cause of Mercutio's death ('My very friend, hath got this mortal hurt / In my behalf') and blames his love of Juliet for making him weak and cowardly.

When Tybalt returns, Romeo is full of anger. The two men fight and Tybalt is killed. Benvolio convinces Romeo to flee for fear of being executed by Prince Escalus.

Romeo leaves as Prince Escalus and the Montague and Capulet parents arrive.

Benvolio explains what has happened. Lady Capulet demands Romeo is executed for killing Tybalt. Lord Montague argues that Romeo was only giving Tybalt the punishment he deserved for killing Mercutio. Prince Escalus announces that Romeo is banished and will be killed if found in Verona.

Act 3 scene 2

Juliet is waiting for night to fall and for Romeo to come and spend their wedding night with her.

The Nurse brings news of Tybalt's death, although Juliet initially thinks it is Romeo who has died until the Nurse explains properly.

Juliet uses a series of oxymorons to show her horror that her husband has killed her cousin ('Dove-feathered raven, wolvish-ravening lamb!') then regrets speaking badly about Romeo and reasons that Tybalt would have killed him.

Her grief for Romeo's banishment is much greater than her grief for Tybalt's death. The Nurse says she will bring Romeo to Juliet.

Key Quotations to Learn

Mercutio: 'I am hurt. / A plague on both your houses.' (IIIi)

Romeo: '... fire-ey'd fury be my conduct now!' (IIIi)

Lady Capulet: 'Prince, as thou art true, / For blood of ours shed blood of Montague.' (IIIi)

Summary

- Tybalt wants to fight with Romeo but he refuses. He refers to, but doesn't reveal, his marriage to Juliet.
- Mercutio is appalled by what he sees as Romeo's cowardice and fights Tybalt himself.
- Romeo tries to stop the fight but Mercutio is killed. In a rage, Romeo kills Tybalt.
- As punishment, Prince Escalus banishes Romeo.
- The Nurse brings news of Tybalt's death and Romeo's exile to Juliet.

Questions

QUICK TEST
1. How do Benvolio and Mercutio's attitudes to fighting appear different in Act 3?
2. In what ways is Romeo partly to blame for Mercutio's death?
3. What misunderstanding is there when the Nurse brings news of what has happened?
4. When she finds out what has happened, what is Juliet's initial attitude towards Romeo and how does this change?

EXAM PRACTICE
Using one or more of the 'Key Quotations to Learn', write a paragraph analysing how violence is presented in Act 3 scene 1.

Act 3 scenes 3 to 5

You must be able to: understand what happens in the second half of Act 3.

Act 3 scene 3

Friar Laurence brings Romeo news of his banishment to Mantua. Romeo says he would rather be dead than be separated from Juliet: 'Tis torture and not mercy. Heaven is here / Where Juliet lives'.

The Nurse arrives and describes Juliet's grief. Romeo considers killing himself and the Friar criticises his rash and unmanly thoughts.

The Friar tells Romeo to go to Juliet. He talks hopefully of a time when the marriage can be revealed, the families united and Romeo pardoned.

Act 3 scene 4

Paris has come to woo Juliet. Lord and Lady Capulet apologise for her absence and explain that she is grieving for her cousin, Tybalt.

Lord Capulet suddenly decides that Juliet will marry Paris in three days' time. He has no doubt that she will do as he wishes and sends his wife to inform Juliet of her wedding.

Act 3 scene 5

Romeo and Juliet have spent their wedding night together. Juliet wants Romeo to stay a little longer. He says he'll stay and face death but she accepts he must go.

The Nurse warns that Lady Capulet is on her way. As Romeo leaves, Juliet has a vision of disaster: 'O God, I have an ill-divining soul! / Methinks I see thee, now thou art so low, / As one dead in the bottom of a tomb'.

Lady Capulet enters and thinks that Juliet is still grieving for Tybalt. However, she shows little sympathy and tells her daughter to stop crying. She talks of the Capulets having revenge on Romeo, and Juliet pretends to agree. Lady Capulet announces Juliet's wedding to Paris and she refuses.

Lord Capulet arrives. He is more sympathetic to Juliet's grief than his wife but, when he finds out that Juliet has refused to marry Paris, he quickly loses his temper. He calls his daughter spoiled, foolish, disobedient and a prostitute.

The Nurse and Lady Capulet try to calm him down but he shouts at them, insults Juliet further and threatens to disown her. He leaves and Lady Capulet follows, telling her daughter, 'Do as thou wilt, for I have done with thee'.

Juliet asks the Nurse for help but the Nurse tells her she should forget Romeo and marry Paris. Juliet pretends to agree. Left alone, she decides to seek Friar Laurence's advice, adding, 'If all else fail, myself have power to die'.

Key Quotations to Learn

Romeo: 'There is no world without Verona's walls / But purgatory, torture, hell itself;' (IIIiii)

Lady Capulet: 'We will have vengeance for it, fear thou not.' (IIIv)

Lord Capulet: 'And you be not, hang! Beg! Starve! Die in the streets! / For by my soul I'll ne'er acknowledge thee,' (IIIv)

Summary

- Romeo is distraught to find out that he has been banished and will never see Juliet again.
- Lord Capulet suddenly decides that Paris may marry Juliet.
- Romeo and Juliet spend their wedding night together. As Romeo leaves, Juliet has a vision of him in a tomb.
- Lady Capulet tells Juliet about the wedding to Paris but she refuses. When Juliet's father finds out, he becomes very angry and threatens to disown his daughter.
- The Nurse suggests that the only thing left for Juliet is to marry Paris. Juliet decides to turn to Friar Laurence for help.

Questions

QUICK TEST
1. What city is Romeo banished to?
2. How is Lord Capulet's attitude to Paris marrying Juliet different in Act 3 compared with Act 1?
3. How do Lord and Lady Capulet respond differently to Juliet's grief?
4. What threat does Lord Capulet make towards Juliet if she will not marry Paris?

EXAM PRACTICE
Using one or more of the 'Key Quotations to Learn', write a paragraph analysing how powerful emotions are presented in the second half of Act 3.

You must be able to: understand what happens in Act 4.

Act 4 scene 1

Paris discusses his marriage to Juliet with Friar Laurence. There is **dramatic irony** in the Friar's words as the audience know that Juliet is already married to Romeo. This continues when Juliet arrives and Paris talks of his love for her; her replies, subtly, refer to her love for Romeo.

Paris leaves the Friar and Juliet alone. She is distressed ('past hope, past cure, past help!') and threatens to kill herself.

The Friar outlines his plan to fake her death: the following night, she should drink a potion that will make her appear dead, and the Friar will write to Romeo so he can take her back to Mantua.

Act 4 scene 2

Lord and Lady Capulet, the Nurse, and various servants are making preparations for the wedding. When Juliet arrives, she apologises to her father for her previous disobedience.

Lord Capulet is very pleased by her good behaviour. However, it leads Lord Capulet to bring forward the wedding by another day (meaning the Friar's letter will not reach Romeo in time).

Act 4 scene 3

Juliet is polite and considerate to her mother and the Nurse. She asks them to leave her on her own for the night.

She is scared by what she is about to do, even fearing that the Friar has given her a poison in order to kill her and cover up the part he played in her marriage to Romeo. She is also terrified by the thought of what it will be like to wake up in the family vault, aware that it will also contain Tybalt's dead body.

Saying Romeo's name, she takes the potion and collapses.

Act 4 scene 4

The following morning, there is a happy **atmosphere** as the Nurse, Lord and Lady Capulet, and the servants busily prepare for the wedding.

Lord Capulet sends the Nurse to wake Juliet while he meets with Paris.

Act 4 scene 5

The Nurse finds Juliet apparently dead, 'Alas, alas! Help, help! My lady's dead!'

Her grief alerts Lady Capulet and then Lord Capulet who both show their distress at their daughter's death.

Friar Laurence arrives with Paris who is also grieved by the death of his intended bride, 'O love! O life! Not life, but love in death!'

The Friar consoles them as if Juliet was really dead and Lord Capulet announces that the wedding will become a funeral.

Key Quotations to Learn

Juliet: 'O, if I wake, shall I not be distraught, / Environed with all these hideous fears,' (IViii)

Lady Capulet: '… My child, my only life. / Revive, look up, or I will die with thee!' (IVv)

Lord Capulet: 'Death, that hath ta'en her hence to make me wail / Ties up my tongue and will not let me speak.' (IVv)

Summary

- Juliet would rather die than marry Paris.
- Friar Laurence comes up with a plan to fake Juliet's death and have Romeo take her to Mantua.
- Juliet pretends to make amends with her parents and the Nurse, then takes the Friar's potion.
- The Nurse discovers Juliet's apparently dead body. Her parents grieve her death and Lord Capulet announces that her wedding will be changed to a funeral.

Questions

QUICK TEST
1. Why do the scenes with Friar Laurence often contain dramatic irony?
2. What is the Friar's plan?
3. What is the first thing that goes wrong in the Friar's plan?
4. What are the contrasting moods of scenes 4 and 5?

EXAM PRACTICE
Using one or more of the 'Key Quotations to Learn', write a paragraph analysing how powerful emotions are presented in Act 4.

You must be able to: understand what happens in Act 5.

Act 5 scene 1

Act 5 begins with a **soliloquy** from Romeo in which he describes a dream he had of Juliet bringing him back from the dead with a kiss.

Romeo's servant, Balthasar, arrives from Verona with news of Juliet's death.

Having received no letters from Friar Laurence, Romeo decides to kill himself at Juliet's side, 'Well, Juliet, I will lie with thee tonight'.

Before making his way back to Verona, he buys poison from an apothecary.

Act 5 scene 2

Friar John tells Friar Laurence that he couldn't deliver the letter to Romeo.

Friar Laurence sends for a crowbar in order to break into the Capulet vault. He plans to let Juliet take refuge with him until Romeo can be contacted.

Act 5 scene 3

Paris and his servant are at Juliet's tomb. Paris lays flowers and then hides when he hears Romeo and Balthasar arrive.

Romeo gives Balthasar a letter to deliver to Lord Montague. He tells his servant that he wants to see his love's face, not revealing his true intention of suicide, and threatens to kill Balthasar if he returns.

As Balthasar leaves, Romeo opens the tomb. Paris believes that Romeo, as a Montague, intends something bad against the Capulet corpses. He tries to apprehend Romeo, who warns him off. They fight and Romeo kills him.

As he dies, Paris asks to be laid in the tomb with Juliet. Realising the identity of the man who was going to marry Juliet, Romeo agrees.

In his soliloquy, Romeo describes the vault, Juliet's dead body and the idea of death. He takes the poison, kisses Juliet, and dies.

Friar Laurence arrives at the vault with Balthasar. The Friar discovers the bodies of Romeo and Paris as Juliet begins to wake up.

He tries to convince Juliet to leave the tomb but she refuses and he leaves alone.

She kisses Romeo, picks up a dagger, and stabs herself. She dies as a group of Watchmen arrive, followed by Prince Escalus.

Lord and Lady Capulet enter the tomb and are horrified by what they see. Lord Montague also arrives, explaining that his wife has died from the grief of Romeo's exile.

The Friar explains what has happened and the Prince blames the parents' behaviour.

Lord Capulet and Lord Montague are reconciled. The Prince ends the play with the words: 'For never was a story of more woe / Than this of Juliet and her Romeo'.

Key Quotations to Learn

Romeo: 'Then I defy you, stars!' (Vi)

Romeo: 'The time and my intents are savage-wild, / More fierce and more inexorable far / Than empty tigers or the roaring sea.' (Viii)

Romeo: 'Death that hath suck'd the honey of thy breath / Hath had no power yet upon thy beauty:' (Viii)

Summary

- Hearing news of Juliet's death, Romeo buys poison and returns to Verona.
- Paris sees Romeo at the tomb. They fight and Paris is killed.
- Romeo lays down next to Juliet and drinks the poison.
- The Friar discovers the bodies as Juliet wakes.
- She kills herself and the scene is revealed to the Capulets and the Montagues who reconcile their differences to **honour** their dead children.

Questions

QUICK TEST
1. What did Romeo dream about and why was it significant?
2. Why doesn't Romeo know about Friar Laurence's plan?
3. How does Romeo die and how does Juliet die?
4. Who does Prince Escalus blame for the deaths of Romeo and Juliet?

EXAM PRACTICE
Using one or more of the 'Key Quotations to Learn', write a paragraph analysing how Romeo's feelings are presented in Act 5.

You must be able to: understand how the story relates to its setting.

What is the play's setting?

Romeo and Juliet is set in the Italian city of Verona. The period is unspecified but different aspects suggest a time around the fourteenth century.

Although the play focuses on two wealthy families, the Capulets and the Montagues, a variety of social groups appear. Prince Escalus and Paris represent other rich families. There are lower-class characters such as the Nurse and the servant, Balthasar. The play also includes the Friars of the local monastery.

How is the role of women significant in the context?

Verona is presented as a **patriarchal** society. This is particularly evident through Lord Capulet: Paris asks his permission to marry Juliet before he even meets her; Capulet makes the decision that Juliet will be married to Paris and threatens to disown her when she refuses to do so; his wife and servants follow his orders.

Fathers always wanted a son to act as their heir but, notably, Lord Capulet's only child is a girl.

Shakespeare's original Elizabethan audience would have shared many of the patriarchal values that are presented in the play but a modern audience is more likely to question them.

How was marriage different to today?

Arranged marriage is quite unusual in modern Europe but it was once an accepted part of life, especially for wealthier families.

Marriage was often seen as a way to further a family's status. Love was a significant part of marriage but it wasn't always the main concern.

Young women were regularly married to much older men who had made their fortunes (it was far rarer than today for wealthy couples to be the same age or for a man to marry an older woman).

Juliet is only thirteen and Lady Capulet says she should be thinking about marriage and children. To a modern audience this seems abnormal but, centuries ago, this was accepted behaviour. When Shakespeare was writing the play, at the end of the sixteenth century, it was usual for girls to marry between the ages of sixteen and eighteen; he is deliberately making Juliet seem young even for his audience at the time.

Is religion important to the context?

Although it is not a religious play, *Romeo and Juliet* includes a lot of religious imagery to emphasise ideas about love and death.

Italy is a strongly Catholic country and the play also uses different features of the Church, such as confession, the wedding ceremony and trust in religious figures like Friar Laurence.

Summary

- The play is set in the Italian city of Verona at an unspecified time, possibly around the fourteenth century.
- The characters come from different social groups: rich, poor and holy.
- Old-fashioned values and gender inequality are important in the play.
- The play features very different attitudes to marriage compared with today. Arranged marriages were typical amongst wealthy families and it was normal for a very young girl to get married.

Questions

QUICK TEST
1. Who represent the rich sections of society in the play?
2. Who reflect the poorer sections of society?
3. How does Lord Capulet represent a patriarchal society?
4. What was often the main reason for marriage amongst wealthy families?

EXAM PRACTICE
In Act 1 scene 2, Lord Capulet discusses Paris's wish to marry Juliet:

Paris: But now, my lord, what say you to my suit?
Capulet: But saying o'er what I have said before:
           My child is yet a stranger in the world;
           She hath not seen the change of fourteen years,
           Let two more summers wither in their pride,
           Ere we may think her ripe to be a bride.
Paris: Younger than she are happy mothers made.
Capulet: And too soon marr'd are those so early made.
           The earth hath swallow'd all my hopes but she,
           She is the hopeful lady of my earth:
           But woo her, gentle Paris, get her heart,
           My will to her consent is but a part;

Write a paragraph explaining how far Paris and Lord Capulet's attitudes towards marriage are presented as typical for the time in which the play is set.

Elizabeth I and Renaissance England

You must be able to: understand how the play reflects the time in which it was written.

When was the play written?

Romeo and Juliet is thought to have been written around 1595 and was one of Shakespeare's most successful plays.

At the time, Italy was considered a very fashionable place by the English and it had a reputation for passionate people and violent family rivalries.

The story isn't true but Shakespeare did borrow the idea from several folk tales and poems.

How does the play reflect Elizabethan England?

Romeo and Juliet is full of different conflicts. This was a familiar scenario in English society, meaning the audience would relate to events in the play.

The previous century had seen the War of the Roses, with two rival families fighting for control of the throne. Although this turbulence had ended, the previous monarch (Henry VIII) had established conflict between Protestant and Catholic families by breaking England away from the Catholic Church.

When Shakespeare was writing the play, there were lots of riots protesting against high taxes and lack of food. He draws on these shocking instances of public chaos and fighting when presenting the Capulet and Montague rivalry spilling onto the streets of Verona, 'What ho! You men, you beasts! / That quench the fire of your pernicious rage / With purple fountains issuing from your veins'.

Plague was a terrible feature of Elizabethan society with major outbreaks in the second half of the sixteenth century. Shakespeare uses plague imagery when Mercutio curses the rival families, as well as using it to explain why the Friar's letter never reaches Romeo.

How might the play have been affected by expectations of Elizabethan theatre?

Elizabethan theatregoers were much more rowdy than modern audiences. Although the play is a tragic love story, Shakespeare includes lots of rude comedy to appeal to the less refined members of his audience. This is most obvious in the character of Mercutio whose dialogue features puns and sexual innuendos, 'Prick love for pricking and you beat love down'.

The Nurse is also a comedy character, possibly made more amusing by being a man in women's clothes. In Shakespeare's time, women could not act on stage so young female roles were taken by boys who had not yet fully grown. However, an older female character might not be carried off as convincingly by a fully-grown man so an actor could play up to all her raunchy lines about men in Act 1 scene 3 or her unintended sexual **double entendres** in Act 2 scene 4.

Summary

- The play is based on an old story about two young lovers.
- The civil conflicts presented on stage would have seemed familiar to its English audience.
- Plague was a terrible feature of Elizabethan England and Shakespeare uses this to heighten the drama.
- Lots of rude jokes are included alongside the tragic romance in order to appeal to the rowdy sixteenth-century audience.

Questions

QUICK TEST
1. Why might Shakespeare have set the play in Italy?
2. What different conflicts had taken place in England's recent history?
3. What is the main dramatic role of characters like Mercutio and the Nurse?
4. What references to plague are included in the play?

EXAM PRACTICE
In Act 1 scene 1, two Capulet servants discuss their rivalry with the Montagues:

Sampson: 'Tis all one, I will show myself a tyrant: when I
            have fought with the men, I will be cruel with the
            maids, and cut off their heads.

Gregory: The heads of the maids?

Sampson: Ay, the heads of the maids, or their maidenheads;
            take it in what sense thou wilt.

Gregory: They must take it in sense that feel it.

Sampson: Me they shall feel while I am able to stand: and
            'tis known I am a pretty piece of flesh.

Gregory: 'Tis well thou art not fish; if thou hadst, thou
            hadst been poor John. Draw thy tool! here comes
            two of the house of the Montagues.

Write a paragraph explaining how Shakespeare uses conflict and sexual humour in this extract to appeal to his audience.

Tragedy and Stagecraft

You must be able to: understand how Shakespeare uses features of genre and stagecraft.

What is a tragedy?

When a play is classed as a tragedy, it usually features tragic events, the downfall of a central character and an unhappy ending.

The opening Prologue tells the audience that they are watching the downfall of Romeo and Juliet. The obstacles that separate the lovers can be considered tragic, as can the deaths of Mercutio and Tybalt, which begin a chain of events that lead to the play's biggest tragedy: Romeo and Juliet's suicides. Shakespeare keeps the ending focussed on their deaths even though the two families finally unite.

Soliloquies

A soliloquy is when a character speaks their thoughts aloud on stage, heard only by the audience. Shakespeare uses soliloquies to intensify the tragic and passionate mood on stage. The important soliloquies in the play come from Juliet in Act 2 scene 5, Act 3 scene 2 and Act 4 scene 3, and from Romeo in Act 5 scenes 1 and 3.

Disguise and concealment

Disguising a character, or a character hiding in order to observe and listen, were key features of Shakespeare's comedies. However, in *Romeo and Juliet*, he uses these techniques to emphasise romance and tragedy.

The masked ball makes clear use of disguise, creating romance between the two main characters who tragically don't realise they are from rival families. It also establishes conflict when Tybalt discovers that Romeo has attended the Capulet feast.

Concealment can be seen in Act 2's balcony scene. Romeo watches Juliet and passionately describes her; unaware of his presence, she freely expresses her love for him. Concealment is also used in Act 5 scene 3, where Paris hides from Romeo and misinterprets his reason for breaking into the Capulet tomb.

Violence and changes in mood

Towards the end of the sixteenth century, theatre audiences wanted more shocks and violence. Shakespeare emphasises his theme of conflict and tragedy with various swordfights and the deaths of Mercutio, Tybalt, Paris, Romeo and Juliet.

Audiences also wanted comedy so, although the play is a tragedy, Shakespeare filled his work with rude puns and sexual innuendos. However, through juxtaposition in the narrative structure, he uses comedy to emphasise the tragedy.

For example, Mercutio's jokes about Benvolio and Tybalt in Act 3 scene 1 mean that the subsequent violence and death that culminate in Romeo's banishment is particularly shocking. Similarly, a light-hearted scene between the Capulets and their servants in Act 4 scene 4 leads into the moving discovery of Juliet's apparently dead body.

Summary

* *Romeo and Juliet* is a tragedy, featuring the key genre elements of tragic events, the downfall of the main characters and an unhappy ending.
* Shakespeare includes comedy to appeal to his audience but carefully structures it in the narrative so that it emphasises the tragedy.
* Soliloquies, disguise and concealment are also used by Shakespeare to emphasise aspects of the play's tragedy and romance.

Questions

QUICK TEST
1. What events in the play can be considered tragic?
2. Which characters perform soliloquies?
3. Which famous scene in the play uses concealment to emphasise romance?
4. Why might Shakespeare have included lots of comedy and violence in the play?

EXAM PRACTICE
In Act 3 scene 2, Juliet awaits her wedding night with Romeo, unaware that he has just killed her cousin:

Juliet: Come, gentle night, come, loving, black-brow'd night,
          Give me my Romeo; and, when he shall die,
          Take him and cut him out in little stars,
          And he will make the face of heaven so fine
          That all the world will be in love with night
          And pay no worship to the garish sun.
          O, I have bought the mansion of a love,
          But not possess'd it, and, though I am sold,
          Not yet enjoy'd: so tedious is this day
          As is the night before some festival
          To an impatient child that hath new robes
          And may not wear them. O, here comes my nurse,
          And she brings news; and every tongue that speaks
          But Romeo's name speaks heavenly eloquence.

Write a paragraph explaining how Shakespeare uses Juliet's soliloquy (above) to create a tragic mood.

You must be able to: analyse how Shakespeare presents Romeo at the start of the play.

What are the audience's first impressions of Romeo?

Romeo is introduced through a conversation between his parents and Benvolio. The natural **imagery** in Lord Montague's description, 'With tears augmenting the fresh morning dew, / Adding to clouds more clouds with his deep sighs' (Ii), present Romeo as a sensitive, romantic young man.

His melancholic, private behaviour is emphasised by images of darkness, 'Shuts up his windows, locks fair daylight out' (Ii).

When he appears on stage in the same scene (Ii), it becomes clear that he is suffering from unrequited love. The **metaphor** 'Griefs of mine own lie heavy in my breast' shows his misery, while a list of oxymorons conveys the painful **duality** of loving someone who doesn't love you back.

He is resolute in his love for Rosaline, 'thou canst not teach me to forget' (Ii). This may make the audience doubtful of his sudden change of heart when he meets Juliet in Act 1 scene 5, although the **rhetorical question** 'Did my heart love till now?' could express his own surprise at experiencing true love.

How does he show his feelings for Juliet?

Romeo shows his romantic character by comparing Juliet to nature, such as 'a snowy dove' (Iv), and using imagery of light, 'Juliet is the sun' (IIii).

There are references to Juliet being heavenly, 'O speak again bright angel' (IIii).

Romeo uses images of value, 'she hangs upon the cheek of the night / As a rich jewel in an Ethiop's ear' (Iv) and 'I should adventure for such merchandise' (IIii).

He displays the courtesy expected of a young man, using religious metaphor, 'If I profane with my unworthiest hand / This holy shrine' (Iv). However, he is also quite forward, with the same imagery continuing when he asks to kiss her, 'My lips, two blushing pilgrims, ready stand / To smooth that rough touch with a tender kiss' (Iv).

Where is he youthful and impetuous?

In Act 2 scene 4, Romeo is shown exchanging witty but childish puns with Mercutio, as well as joining in with his sexual innuendos, 'Why, then is my pump well flowered'.

He is also presented as impulsive when he climbs the walls into the Capulets' garden in order to see Juliet, despite the threat of death, and in his readiness to marry Juliet less than a day after meeting her.

Key Quotations to Learn

'She hath forsworn to love, and in that vow / Do I live dead, that live to tell it now.' (Ii)

'One fairer than my love! The all seeing sun / Ne'er saw her match since first the world begun.' (Iii)

'With love's light wings did I o'erperch these walls, / For stony limits cannot hold love out,' (IIii)

Summary

- Romeo is presented as being romantic and melancholy, suffering from unrequited love for Rosaline.
- He is respectful, courteous and romantic towards Juliet.
- Romeo has a lively side to his character, swapping jokes with Mercutio.
- He also shows the impetuousness of youth when he risks death to see Juliet and rushes into marriage.

Sample Analysis

Shakespeare initially presents Romeo as romantic and melancholy. Romeo uses the metaphor, 'I am too sore enpierced with his shaft / To soar with his light feathers', when Mercutio uses Cupid imagery to encourage him to enjoy himself. The **verb** 'enpierced' emphasises the pain Romeo feels from his unrequited love for Rosaline. The use of the **homophone** sore/soar hints at Romeo's witty, playful side but focuses on how downcast he feels; this willingness to wallow in his misery also implies a childish, self-indulgent side to his character. The reference to Cupid's 'light feathers' suggests he feels a bitter irony at what love should be like compared with its current unhappy reality.

Questions

QUICK TEST
1. What behaviour of Romeo's does Lord Montague describe and what is its cause?
2. How might his love for Rosaline lead an audience to criticise Romeo later in the play?
3. What different imagery does Romeo use to describe Juliet?
4. What evidence is there of Romeo behaving rashly?

EXAM PRACTICE
Using one or more of the 'Key Quotations to Learn', write a paragraph analysing how Shakespeare presents the romantic side of Romeo's character.

Romeo's Development

You must be able to: analyse how Shakespeare presents Romeo later in the play.

How does Shakespeare present a more mature Romeo?

Romeo seems more sensible during his confrontation with Tybalt in Act 3 scene 1, but Mercutio interprets this as a lack of honour.

Romeo excuses Tybalt's aggression and walks away: 'villain am I none, / Therefore farewell. I see thou knowest me not'. Despite Tybalt demanding a duel, Romeo defends himself with words, 'I do protest I never injured thee, / But love thee better than thou canst devise'.

Shakespeare uses dramatic irony to show that this change is due to his secret marriage to Juliet, 'Till thou shalt know the reason of my love'.

How does Romeo react to Mercutio's murder?

After Mercutio's death, Romeo reflects on his changed behaviour, using metaphor to suggest that he has become unmanly and dishonourable, 'Thy beauty hath made me effeminate / And in my temper softened valour's steel'.

He is full of anger and returns to his previous recklessness. When he fights with Tybalt, he doesn't appear to care whether he dies, stating that someone must accompany Mercutio to heaven: 'Either thou, or I, or both must go with him'.

What is Romeo's response to being banished?

In earlier scenes, when describing his unrequited love, Romeo uses death imagery as romantic **hyperbole**. This returns in Act 3, as Romeo compares exile from Juliet with feelings of torture and death.

Shakespeare also begins to use death imagery to suggest Romeo's dangerous lack of regard for his own life, 'Banishment! Be merciful, say "death". / For exile have more terror in his look'. Similarly, after his wedding night with Juliet, he is easily convinced to remain with her, 'I have more care to stay than will to go. / Come death, and welcome'.

How is Romeo presented in the final act?

When Romeo is brought news of Juliet's apparent death, his response is very brief to suggest shock and disbelief: 'Is it e'en so?'

He instantly makes a plan to kill himself by Juliet's side, referring to himself as 'life-weary' when buying the poison. He does not share his intentions with anyone and his resolution is clear when he threatens to kill Balthasar if he disturbs him ('By heaven I will tear thee joint by joint').

He reluctantly kills Paris, then shows **empathy** and honour when he lays him in the tomb.

Shakespeare uses repeated **personification** of death to show Romeo's feelings of despair. Struck by Juliet's beauty, he drinks the poison, kisses her and dies.

Key Quotations to Learn

'Calling death 'banished' / Thou cut'st my head off with a golden axe / And smilest upon the stroke that murders me.' (IIIiii)

[Describing the tomb and his plan to kill himself] 'Thus I enforce thy rotten jaws to open, / And in despite I'll cram thee with more food.' (Viii)

'And lips, O you / The doors of breath, seal with a righteous kiss / A dateless bargain to engrossing Death.' (Viii)

Summary

- Romeo seems sensible and mature when he tries to avoid conflict with Tybalt.
- After Mercutio's death, he blames his love of Juliet for making him weak.
- He becomes increasingly reckless: killing Tybalt, lingering in Juliet's room after the wedding night and deciding to kill himself for Juliet.
- He displays an honourable side when he lays Paris to rest in Juliet's tomb.
- Romeo's love for Juliet continues to his death.

Sample Analysis

Romeo's love for Juliet can be seen when he says, 'For here lies Juliet, and her beauty makes / This vault a feasting presence full of light', describing how she makes the tomb seem like a room in a palace (a presence chamber). This **regal** imagery suggests how highly he values her as well as the way in which she rules his heart, linking to how he has come to the tomb to die by her side. The metaphor also suggests he sees Juliet's beauty as a source of wonder and holiness. The implied darkness of the 'vault' is contrasted with 'light' and this duality reflects the romance and tragedy of love that the two main characters encapsulate during the play.

Questions

QUICK TEST
1. Why does Romeo not want to fight Tybalt?
2. What does Romeo compare his banishment with?
3. What technique does Shakespeare use in Romeo's final speech to show despair?
4. Who does he tell about his plan to kill himself by Juliet's side?

EXAM PRACTICE
Using one or more of the 'Key Quotations to Learn', write a paragraph analysing how Shakespeare uses images of death to present aspects of Romeo's character.

Juliet

You must be able to: analyse how Shakespeare presents Juliet at the start of the play.

What are the audience's first impressions of Juliet?

At the start of the play, Shakespeare emphasises Juliet's youth.

As with Lord Montague discussing Romeo, Juliet is introduced through her father. In Act 1 scene 2 he tells Paris, 'She hath not seen the change of fourteen years', and reveals that she is an only child.

Juliet appears in the next scene, alongside Lady Capulet and the Nurse who have a similar discussion about her age.

She appears to have little interest in love or marriage ('It is an honour that I dream not of') until she meets Romeo.

How does she show her feelings for Romeo?

Although Romeo instigates their relationship, Juliet readily encourages him and mirrors his use of religious imagery, 'For saints have hands that pilgrims' hands do touch, / And palm to palm is holy palmers' kiss'.

Later, talking to herself on her balcony, Juliet implies that she would give up everything for Romeo, 'be but sworn my love / And I'll no longer be a Capulet'.

She is embarrassed to find Romeo has overheard her, 'a maiden blush bepaint my cheek', but she says she doesn't deny her feelings for him.

Juliet also seems uncertain of her behaviour. She tells Romeo to swear he loves her then uses the **simile** 'too like the lightning' to show her fears that they are rushing their romance and it may not last.

She describes her love as 'deep' and 'infinite' and says that she will honour and obey Romeo. While saying she cannot bear to be parted from Romeo, she also acknowledges the power her love has over him, comparing herself to a prisoner keeping a bird on a string: 'And with a silken thread plucks it back again, / So loving-jealous of his liberty'.

Like Romeo, she also uses images of death to convey the strength of her love. For example, when Romeo says he would happily be her pet bird, she adds, 'Sweet, so would I: / Yet I should kill thee with much cherishing'.

Does Juliet seem rebellious or obedient?

Juliet speaks very little in her first scene, giving brief answers but allowing her mother and nurse to dominate the conversation. After her mother's insistence about getting married, she agrees to consider Paris as a suitor.

However, when Romeo comes to her balcony, she encourages him rather than calling her family, and it is she who suggests that they marry the following day.

Key Quotations to Learn

'O Romeo, Romeo, wherefore art thou Romeo? / Deny thy father and refuse thy name.' (IIii)

'... thou overhead'st, ere I was ware, / My true-love passion;' (IIii)

'And all my fortunes at thy foot I'll lay, / And follow thee my lord throughout the world.' (IIii)

Summary

- Shakespeare emphasises Juliet's youth and she initially seems obedient.
- She appears to have no wish to get married.
- She encourages Romeo's love, even after finding out that he is a Montague.
- Despite some caution about Romeo's faithfulness, Juliet confesses her love and suggests that they get married.

Sample Analysis

Shakespeare presents Juliet as initially doubting Romeo, 'Yet, if thou swear'st, / Thou may prove false [...] O gentle Romeo, / If thou dost love, pronounce it faithfully', suggesting she feels cautious about their relationship. The verbs 'swear' and 'pronounce' show her eagerness to be with Romeo, as does the approving **adjective** 'gentle'. This is emphasised by the **imperative** sentence, suggesting a desperation to believe that he loves her. However, the contrast between 'false' and 'faithfully' displays her inner conflict, and her doubt can also be seen in her language of uncertainty, such as 'if' and 'may'.

Questions

QUICK TEST
1. How old is Juliet?
2. What makes her seem obedient?
3. What sacrifice does she say she would make to be with Romeo?
4. What similar imagery do Juliet and Romeo use to describe love?

EXAM PRACTICE
Using one or more of the 'Key Quotations to Learn', write a paragraph analysing how Shakespeare presents Juliet's feelings for Romeo.

Juliet's Development

You must be able to: analyse how Shakespeare presents Juliet later in the play.

How does Juliet respond to the events surrounding Tybalt's death?

At first, Juliet believes Romeo has been killed. Short sentences and **repetition**, 'O break, my heart. Poor bankrupt, break at once' emphasise her heartache.

A rhetorical question and oxymorons show her horror that Romeo has murdered her cousin, 'Did ever dragon keep so fair a cave? / Beautiful tyrant, fiend angelical'.

Reasoning that Tybalt would have killed Romeo, she reproaches herself and a list of infinite measurements conveys the extent of her despair: 'Romeo is banished, / There is no end, no limit, measure, bound, / In that word's death'.

In what ways is Juliet presented as being alone?

Several scenes feature Juliet alone, such as waiting for the Nurse in Act 2 scene 5, waiting for Romeo in Act 3 scene 2 and taking the Friar's potion in Act 4 scene 3.

When she believes she will spend her wedding night alone, her use of death imagery continues: 'death, not Romeo take my maidenhead'.

Juliet later finds herself at variance with her mother. As Lady Capulet talks of having Romeo killed, Juliet uses pause and double meaning to offer a veiled support of the man she loves: 'Indeed I never shall be satisfied / With Romeo, till I behold him – dead – / Is my poor heart so for a kinsman vexed'.

This family division increases when both parents seem to disown her, 'O sweet my mother, cast me not away'. After the Nurse advises her to forget Romeo, she decides never to confide in her again, 'Go, counsellor. / Thou and my bosom henceforth shall be twain'.

Where does Juliet seem more headstrong?

Juliet's strong-minded nature can be seen in how she expresses her refusal to marry: 'I will not marry yet. And when I do, I swear / It shall be Romeo, whom you know I hate, / Rather than Paris'.

Her faithfulness to Romeo makes her bold. In Act 4 scene 1, she threatens to kill herself then lists horrible scenarios that she would accept over marrying Paris, 'And I will do it without fear or doubt, / To live an unstain'd wife to my sweet love'.

How is Juliet presented in the final act?

Waking in Act 5 scene 3, Juliet refuses to leave with the Friar. She maintains her former wish to be with Romeo or die, and Shakespeare dramatises this clash of romance and tragedy with her attempt to kiss poison from Romeo's lips.

Key Quotations to Learn

'Just opposite to what thou justly seem'st! / A damned saint, an honourable villain!' (IIIii)

'Twixt my extremes and me this bloody knife / Shall play the umpire,' (IVi)

'O happy dagger. / This is thy sheath. There rust, and let me die.' (Viii)

Summary

- Juliet goes through conflicting feelings after Tybalt's death: first thinking Romeo has died, then being horrified by Romeo's actions, before reproaching herself and finally feeling despair at his banishment.
- Her relationship with her parents is destroyed when she refuses to marry Paris.
- Her loneliness is complete when she feels she cannot rely on her nurse for support.
- Juliet's faithfulness to Romeo makes her strong-willed and reckless. She threatens to kill herself before undertaking the Friar's plan to fake her own death.

Sample Analysis

Juliet's love for Romeo can be seen when she says, 'Love, lord, ay husband, friend, / I must hear from thee every day in the hour, / For in a minute there are many days' as he leaves to begin his exile in Mantua. The list of titles shows the strength of their relationship by presenting it as multi-faceted and displaying emotion, respect and intimacy. Despite the inclusion of 'lord', implying **traditional** expectations of an obedient wife, the list creates a sense of equality between the two lovers. Her sadness at being parted from Romeo is conveyed through metaphor, suggesting that time without him will be an eternity. This combination of dependency and desire is emphasised by the imperative verb 'I must' and her hyperbolic demand to hear from him hourly.

Questions

QUICK TEST
1. What does Juliet's mother plan for Romeo?
2. What does the Nurse say that makes Juliet feel betrayed and unsupported?
3. What is Juliet determined to do in terms of her marriage to Romeo?
4. How does Juliet first try to kill herself when she finds Romeo dead?

EXAM PRACTICE
Using one or more of the 'Key Quotations to Learn', write a paragraph analysing how Shakespeare presents Juliet's emotions in the second half of the play.

Mercutio

You must be able to: analyse how Shakespeare presents the character of Mercutio.

How does Shakespeare make Mercutio a comic character?

Mercutio is Romeo's friend and his rude humour would have been popular with Shakespeare's original audience.

He often repeats Romeo's words, using punning to change them into sexual innuendo. For example, when Romeo describes his feelings for Rosaline as, 'Under love's heavy burden do I sink', Mercutio replies: 'And, to sink in it, should you burden love – / Too great oppression for a tender thing'. The words 'it' and 'tender thing' refer to Rosaline's vagina. Mercutio changes the meaning of 'sink in' to suggest sexual intercourse, and 'burden' to mean the weight of Romeo on top of Rosaline.

He makes a lot of penis jokes. When Romeo describes the pain of unrequited love, 'pricks like thorn', Mercutio uses 'prick' as slang for the penis. He tells Romeo to 'prick love', suggesting sexual intercourse, and describes how you can 'beat love down', implying forgetting Rosaline and lowering an erection.

Sexual humour continues throughout Mercutio's scenes:

- He describes the fairy Queen Mab teaching virgins to become pregnant, 'learns them first to bear' (Iiv).
- He links Romeo and Rosaline to the medlar fruit, which was considered to look like a vagina, 'Now he will sit under a medlar tree, / And wish his mistress were that kind of fruit' (Iii).
- He jokes the Nurse is a prostitute by turning a description of the time into a reference to masturbation, 'for the bawdy hand of the dial is now upon the prick of noon' (IIiv).

How is his death tragic?

At the start of Act 3 scene 1, Mercutio is joking with Benvolio. He is reckless ('By my heel, I care not') and the humorous mood quickly changes. His mockery of Tybalt turns into an argument, brandishing his sword after taking offence at Tybalt's word 'consortest', which implies being a lower-class musician, 'Here's my fiddlestick, here's that shall make you dance. Zounds, consort!'

When Romeo will not draw his sword, Mercutio is disappointed in him and fights Tybalt himself. He is stabbed when Romeo tries to hold him back to keep the peace. Shakespeare creates further tragic irony through the fatal 'scratch' linking back to Mercutio's previous use of the word 'prick'.

His humour continues but is full of death imagery, 'Ask for me tomorrow and you will find me a grave man'.

He blames his friend ('why the devil came you between us? I was hurt under your arm') and dies, cursing both the Montagues and the Capulets.

Key Quotations to Learn

[Mercutio describing Rosaline] 'By her fine foot, straight leg, and quivering thigh, / And the demesnes that there adjacent lie,' (Iii, demesnes = a piece of land for ploughing)

[The Nurse, about Mercutio] '... what saucy merchant was this, that was so full of his ropery?' (IIiv, ropery = rude jokes)

'They have made worms' meat of me.' (IIIi)

Summary

- Mercutio is Romeo's friend.
- His rude humour would have made the character popular with Elizabethan audiences.
- He uses puns to change Romeo's words into sexual innuendos.
- The mood of his final scene turns from comic into tragic.
- Romeo is the accidental cause of his death and he dies cursing the two rival families.

Sample Analysis

Mercutio is presented as a tragic figure in Act 3 scene 1. His humour continues even after he is stabbed by Tybalt, 'tis not so deep as a well, nor so wide as a church door, but tis enough, twill serve' but is now blackened by references to death. His familiar technique of punning appears in the double meaning of 'well', describing the shallowness of the wound while implying how badly it has injured him. In the second simile to describe his injury, the church reference suggests that he will soon need a funeral. Despite his jokes, it is clear that he knows he is going to die, 'tis enough, twill serve'. His speech also creates tragic irony because these repeated references to the seeming slightness of the cut link back to his earlier sexual innuendos based around the word 'prick'.

Questions

QUICK TEST
1. What is a pun?
2. What are most of Mercutio's jokes about?
3. How does Romeo accidentally cause Mercutio's death?
4. How is Mercutio's language in his final, dying speeches similar and different to his dialogue in previous scenes?

EXAM PRACTICE
Using one or more of the 'Key Quotations to Learn', write a paragraph analysing how Shakespeare presents the character of Mercutio.

Tybalt

You must be able to: analyse how Shakespeare presents the character of Tybalt.

How is Tybalt presented as aggressive?

Tybalt represents the hostility between the Capulets and the Montagues. His first words are to Benvolio, who is trying to stop a fight between the families' servants: 'What, art thou drawn among these heartless hinds? / Turn thee, Benvolio, and look upon thy death'. Animal imagery implies the lowliness of the servants and he insultingly groups Benvolio among them before threatening to kill him.

He seems like a villain and this is emphasised when he says he hates peace and calls Benvolio a coward. However, in Act 3 scene 1, he is polite, 'Gentlemen, good e'en […] peace be with you', and initially avoids fighting Mercutio, 'What wouldst thou have with me?'

How does Shakespeare establish Tybalt's grudge against Romeo?

In Act 3 scene 1, Tybalt challenges Romeo to a duel, saying, 'Boy, this shall not excuse the injuries / That thou hast done me, therefore turn and draw'. He tries to demean Romeo by addressing him as 'Boy', and his dislike goes back to the Capulet feast in Act 1 scene 5.

Furious at a Montague attending the party, he asks himself how Romeo could dare 'fleer and scorn at our solemnity'. He sees himself as superior, referring to Romeo as a 'slave' and judging his presence an insult to 'the stock and honour of my kin'.

He repeatedly refers to Romeo as a 'villain' and his anger increases when Lord Capulet stops him from starting a fight. He is humiliated when Lord Capulet shouts at him and it is implied that he blames Romeo, describing his new grievance against him as 'bitt'rest gall'.

How is Tybalt presented through the opinions of others?

Mercutio clearly dislikes Tybalt. Talking to Benvolio in Act 2 scene 4, he mocks Tybalt's skill as a swordsman ('he fights as you sing pricksongs') and is sarcastic about his social status ('a gentleman of the very first house'). He uses **alliteration** to emphasise his ironic praise of Tybalt's honourable qualities: 'Prince of Cats. O, he's the courageous captain of compliments'.

Lord Capulet describes Tybalt as a disobedient child ('You are a saucy boy. […] You are a princox'). However, he later says, '[Juliet] lov'd her kinsman Tybalt dearly, / And so did I'.

The Nurse and Juliet also speak fondly of Tybalt after his death. The Nurse refers to him as 'O courteous Tybalt, honest gentleman', while Juliet calls him her 'dearest cousin'.

Key Quotations to Learn

[About killing Romeo] 'To strike him dead I hold it not a sin.' (Iv)

'Romeo the love I bear thee can afford / No better term than this: thou art a villain.' (IIIi)

[Threatening to kill Romeo, having just killed Mercutio] 'Thou wretched boy, that didst consort him here, / Shalt with him hence.' (IIIi)

Summary

- Tybalt bears a grudge against Romeo for attending the Capulet feast.
- He is aggressive and represents the hostility between the two families.
- He comes into conflict with Lord Capulet and is humbled by him.
- He has a courteous side and, after his death, the Capulets speak highly of him.

Sample Analysis

Tybalt's youthful arrogance and aggression can be seen in his conflict with Lord Capulet in Act 1 scene 5:

Tybalt: I'll not endure him.
Lord Capulet: He shall be endur'd.
                   What goodman boy! I say he shall!

His anger and lack of tolerance can be seen in his refusal to 'endure' Romeo; this verb also implies that he sees himself as superior to the Montagues. Lord Capulet sees this as a challenge to his own esteem, so interrupts him and reproachfully copies his language. He also mirrors Tybalt's use of modality by using, and then repeating, the **modal verb** 'shall' to emphasise his own authority. The exclamation marks suggest Lord Capulet should be shouting down Tybalt's insolence and he humiliates him further by belittling his masculinity ('boy') and his social status ('goodman', a term linked to farmers and tradesmen).

Questions

QUICK TEST
1. In his first scene on stage, what does Tybalt say he hates?
2. What word does he repeatedly use to describe Romeo?
3. What qualities of Tybalt does the Nurse mention after his death?

EXAM PRACTICE
Using one or more of the 'Key Quotations to Learn', write a paragraph analysing how Shakespeare presents Tybalt's hatred of Romeo.

Lord and Lady Capulet

You must be able to: analyse how Shakespeare presents Juliet's parents.

How is Lord Capulet presented at the start of the play?

Lord Capulet is presented as aggressive, 'Give me my long sword [...] My sword I say!' with repetition emphasising his eagerness to fight.

He seems calmer in the next scene, ''tis not hard I think / For men so old as we to keep the peace'. This could be genuine, due to the Prince's warning, or just to make a good impression on Paris. He is aggressive again in Act 1 scene 5, when Tybalt disobeys him, which may suggest he is only calm when getting his way.

Capulet is protective of his daughter, 'My child is yet a stranger in this world', and cautious of an early marriage. He appears unusually respectful of his daughter's right to choose a husband, although she only seems expected to choose from the men he selects.

How does Lady Capulet seem different to her husband?

Lady Capulet is first shown mocking her husband by pointing out his age and infirmity, 'A crutch! A crutch! Why call you for a sword?'

She appears irresponsible over Juliet's future, 'Well, think on marriage now'. The imperative suggests an impatience that seems based on personal experience, 'I was your mother much upon these years / That you are now a maid'.

As part of this pressure, she is romantic, saying of Paris, 'Verona's summer hath not such a flower' before describing, in sonnet form, the wonders of love.

How do Lord and Lady Capulet change?

They are changed by Tybalt's death; she is more aggressive, demanding Romeo's execution and planning his murder, while her husband (perhaps struck by the brevity of life, 'Well we were born to die') suddenly decides Juliet should marry Paris.

Whereas Lady Capulet is dismissive of Juliet's grief, Lord Capulet is caring and compares her to a boat in a storm. However, when she refuses to marry Paris, Shakespeare uses a range of techniques to show Capulet's anger: rhetorical questions ('Doth she not give us thanks?'), mimicry ('"Proud" and "I thank you"'), insults ('you green-sickness carrion!'), threats ('you shall not house with me'), orders and **patterns of three** ('Speak not, reply not, do not answer me') and curses ('God's bread, it makes me mad!').

Both parents wish Juliet dead and are then full of grief when they believe she has died in Act 4 scene 5. At the end of the play, Lord Capulet makes the first gesture of friendship, 'O brother Montague, give me thy hand'.

Key Quotations to Learn

Lord Capulet: 'too soon marr'd are those so early made.' (Iii)

Lady Capulet: 'Read o'er the volume of young Paris' face / And find delight writ there with beauty's pen.' (Iiii)

Lady Capulet: 'I would the fool were married to her grave!' (IIIv)

Lord Capulet: 'Death lies on her like an untimely frost / Upon the sweetest flower of all the field.' (IVv)

Summary

- Despite talking calmly to Paris, Lord Capulet often seems angry and aggressive.
- He expresses his love for Juliet but treats her cruelly when she disobeys him.
- Lady Capulet seems irresponsible in her wish to see Juliet married and pregnant.
- Like her husband, she later wishes Juliet dead.
- They are distraught when they find Juliet apparently dead. After discovering her true death, Lord Capulet moves to reconcile with the Montagues.

Sample Analysis

Lord Capulet's flaws as a parent can be seen in Act 3 scene 4. He says to Paris, 'I think she will be rul'd / In all respects by me; nay, more, I doubt it not', as he makes his sudden decision that Juliet will be married. His attitude is a sharp contrast to his words to Paris in Act 1 scene 2, conveying how dangerously impulsive he can be. Capulet's pride in his authority is expressed through the **verb phrase** 'rul'd in all respects', showing that, despite earlier seeming to respect his daughter's views, he matches the patriarchal expectations of the time. He can also be seen as eager to show this authority off to Paris, altering the insecure verb 'think' to the more certain 'doubt it not'. It is partly this arrogant certainty that leads him to be so angry when Juliet refuses to marry.

Questions

QUICK TEST
1. Why might Lord Capulet appear much calmer when talking to Paris in Act 1 scene 2?
2. What reason does Lady Capulet appear to have for wanting Juliet to get married?
3. What does Lord Capulet suddenly change his mind about?

EXAM PRACTICE
Using one or more of the 'Key Quotations to Learn', write a paragraph analysing how Shakespeare presents Lord or Lady Capulet's attitude towards Juliet.

The Nurse and Paris

You must be able to: analyse how Shakespeare presents the Nurse and Paris.

In what ways is the Nurse a comic character?

The Nurse has lots of rude jokes, for example not being able to claim she was still a virgin when she was thirteen ('Now by my maidenhead at twelve year old') and using a pun to describe Juliet having sex ('you shall bear the burden soon at night').

Her language is coarse, such as comparing one of Juliet's childhood injuries to a chicken's testicle ('a bump as big as a young cockerel's stone'). She also has fun annoying Juliet by prevaricating in Act 2 scene 5: 'Your love says like an honest gentleman, / And a courteous, and a kind, and a handsome, / And I warrant a virtuous – Where is your mother?'

The Nurse is also made fun of by others. Mercutio suggests she is a prostitute and calls her ugly, 'hide her face'. When she tells her servant off for letting Mercutio 'use me at his pleasure', Peter turns 'use' into a pun for sex and says he would have joined in, 'I saw no man use you at his pleasure; if I had, my weapon should quickly have been out'.

How else does Shakespeare present the Nurse?

The Nurse has a more serious side. Her own daughter, who would have been Juliet's age, is dead, perhaps explaining her deep affection for Juliet, 'Thou wast the prettiest babe that e'er I nurs'd'.

Although she warns Romeo not to hurt Juliet, the Nurse seems excited to see them falling in love ('Lord, Lord, she will be a joyful woman') and acts as their go-between.

She is also practical, 'Then, since the case so stands now as it doth, / think it best you married with the County'. It is this advice to marry Paris that makes Juliet feel betrayed.

What is Paris like in the play?

Paris is presented as a good, honourable man. Lady Capulet calls him 'valiant' and the Nurse uses a metaphor to suggest he is perfect, 'he's a man of wax'.

He is loving towards Juliet, 'Poor soul, thy face is much abus'd with tears', and clearly distraught when she is found apparently dead, 'Beguil'd, divorced, wronged, spited, slain. / Most detestable Death, by thee beguil'd'.

He attacks Romeo only to protect Juliet's dead body. It is a sign of Paris's virtue that, when Romeo realises who he is, his dead body is lain in Juliet's tomb.

Key Quotations to Learn

Nurse: 'Go, girl, seek happy nights to happy days.' (Iiii)

Nurse: '... if ye should lead her in a fool's paradise, as they say, it were a very gross kind of behaviour, as they say; for the gentlewoman is young;' (IIiv)

Nurse: 'Romeo's a dishclout to him. An eagle, madam, / Hath not so green, so quick, so fair an eye / As Paris hath. Beshrew my very heart, / I think you are happy in this second match,' (IIIv)

Summary

- The Nurse is a comic character, making rude jokes and being mocked by others.
- She has a serious side. She is affectionate and protective towards Juliet, acting as the go-between for her and Romeo.
- Juliet feels betrayed by the Nurse's practical suggestion that she marries Paris after Romeo's exile.
- Paris is presented as a good, honourable man.

Sample Analysis

When Paris visits Juliet's tomb in Act 5 scene 3, his soliloquy, 'Sweet flower, with flowers thy bridal bed I strew. / [...] Which with sweet water nightly I will dew', contains natural imagery to express his love. Flowers are a traditional symbol of romance and Paris's opening image conveys his feelings for Juliet, emphasised by the repetition of the affectionate adjective 'sweet'. 'Dew' is used to **symbolise** his tears of grief and the **adverb** 'nightly' presents Paris as a constant, honourable lover. Unaware of her true feelings, he sees Juliet as his wife even though they never married and this dramatic irony makes him a tragic figure.

Questions

QUICK TEST
1. How does the Nurse annoy Juliet in Act 2 scene 5?
2. Why might the Nurse feel such strong affection for Juliet?
3. What warning does the Nurse give to Romeo?
4. Which characters particularly praise Paris?

EXAM PRACTICE
Using one or more of the 'Key Quotations to Learn', write a paragraph analysing how Shakespeare presents the Nurse's feelings towards Juliet.

Benvolio and Friar Laurence

You must be able to: analyse how Shakespeare presents the characters of Benvolio and Friar Laurence.

Is Benvolio a typical Montague?

Benvolio is presented as peaceful. He is introduced trying to stop a fight and even asks Tybalt to help, 'I do but keep the peace, put up thy sword, / Or manage it to part these men with me'.

Similarly, at the start of Act 3, he wants to go home because 'the Capels are abroad, / And if we meet we shall not 'scape a brawl'.

However, Mercutio accuses him of being, 'as hot a Jack in thy mood as any in Italy', saying he is easily provoked and that his head is 'full of quarrels'.

What is Benvolio's relationship with Romeo?

Benvolio and Romeo share a melancholy mood, with Benvolio describing his own 'troubled mind' and wish to be alone.

He feels sorry for Romeo, 'I rather weep / [...] At thy good heart's oppression', and understands Romeo's feelings of unrequited love, 'Alas that love so gentle in his view / Should be so tyrannous'. He encourages Romeo to forget Rosaline.

He later defends Romeo to the Prince, 'With gentle breath, calm voice, knees humbly bow'd / Could not take truce with the unruly spleen / Of Tybalt'. However, he omits Mercutio's role in starting the fight and Lady Capulet insists, 'Affection makes him false'.

How is Friar Laurence presented?

Although Friar Laurence's motive is to unite the two families, his actions are questionable. He is surprised by Romeo's altered affections ('And art thou chang'd?') but agrees to wed him to Juliet that afternoon despite his own advice, 'Wisely and slow; they stumble that run fast'.

He has a relaxed attitude to religion, joking that Romeo has slept with Rosaline and uttering blasphemous expressions, 'Holy Saint Francis! / [...] Jesu Maria!'

Before the ceremony, his words **foreshadow** the play's tragedy: 'So smile the heavens upon this holy act / That after hours with sorrow chide us not'.

He later gives Romeo refuge, encouraging him to see banishment as 'mercy' and convincing him not to kill himself. He also stops Juliet from killing herself by proposing that they fake her death.

When he goes to collect Juliet from the tomb himself, it is unclear how far he acts out of care or self-interest: 'Come, I'll dispose of thee / Among a sisterhood of nuns. / [...] I dare no longer stay'.

Taken before the Prince, he says his actions were wrong but had good intentions: 'Myself condemned and myself excus'd'.

Key Quotations to Learn

Benvolio: 'Compare her face with some that I shall show / And I will make thee think thy swan a crow.' (Iii)

Friar Laurence: 'These violent delights have violent ends.' (IIvi)

Friar Laurence: 'Wilt thou slay thyself? / And slay thy lady that in thy life lives, / By doing damned hate upon thyself?' (IIIiii)

Summary

- Benvolio seems more peaceful than most of the young Montagues and Capulets, although Mercutio says he is just as hot-headed.
- Benvolio is close to Romeo and sympathises with his melancholy moods.
- The Friar hopes to bring the families together through Romeo and Juliet's marriage.
- Friar Laurence is always trying to help the young lovers but often seems to make matters worse.

Sample Analysis

Friar Laurence values life and tells Romeo, 'A pack of blessings light upon thy back; / Happiness courts thee in her best array', to discourage him from killing himself. The metaphor tries to make Romeo think more positively by suggesting that the feelings that currently oppress him are better than he thinks, linking to the Friar's belief that banishment is better than execution. The use of the **abstract noun** 'blessings' suggests the Friar sees banishment as a merciful gift from God, a stark contrast to Romeo's suicidal thoughts that were considered a **sin**. Personification is used to emphasise the Friar's attempt to comfort and enliven Romeo, possibly using the female image alongside the verb 'court' to remind him that Juliet is waiting for their wedding night.

Questions

QUICK TEST
1. Who does Benvolio ask to help him stop the fight in Act 1 scene 1?
2. Why does Lady Capulet think Benvolio is lying to Prince Escalus about Tybalt's death?
3. What advice of his own does the Friar appear to ignore when agreeing to marry Romeo to Juliet?
4. Why does the Friar suggest that he and Juliet fake her death?

EXAM PRACTICE
Using one or more of the 'Key Quotations to Learn', write a paragraph analysing how Shakespeare presents Benvolio or the Friar's advice to Romeo.

Love

You must be able to: analyse how Shakespeare explores the theme of love.

How does Shakespeare present true love?

Religious images convey love's purity. Romeo's words suggest Juliet is a holy figure that he worships, 'And touching hers, make blessed my rude hand'. He refers to her as 'dear saint', while she calls him 'good pilgrim'. Shakespeare repeats images of hands and lips to create intimacy and symbolise connection.

Love is personified as a guiding force that leads Romeo to Juliet ('He lent me counsel'). Furthermore, Juliet's metaphor, 'But my true love is grown to such excess / I cannot sum up sum of half my wealth' presents love as a source of great richness that is impossible to measure.

However, love is also presented as feeling too good to be true, 'I am afeard, / Being in night, all this is but a dream, / Too flattering sweet to be substantial', and the opening prologue establishes that their true love is doomed.

Love is linked to feelings of invincibility ('And what love can do, that dares love attempt') when Romeo climbs the wall into the Capulet grounds, and to rash or extreme behaviour, such as the sudden decision to marry or their readiness to kill themselves later in the play.

Ultimately, true love is presented as eternal, with Romeo and Juliet reunited only in death, 'O here / Will I set up my everlasting rest / And shake the yoke of inauspicious stars / From this world-wearied flesh'.

What obstacles to love does Shakespeare explore?

Romeo and Juliet's warring families are presented as an obstacle to love, 'Tis but thy name that is my enemy / [...] If they do see thee, they will murder thee'. This poses both a theoretical and a physical obstacle through Juliet questioning why she shouldn't love a Montague and the genuine danger to Romeo's life.

Other obstacles include Romeo's banishment and Paris's wish to marry Juliet, 'O God, O Nurse, how shall this be prevented? / My husband is on earth, my faith in heaven'.

How is love emphasised by Shakespeare's use of form?

Several characters speak in sonnet form. This is most obvious in the Prologue and in Romeo and Juliet's shared dialogue in Act 1 scene 5.

It can also be seen when Lady Capulet describes Paris in Act 1 scene 3, and Romeo's attempts to use the sonnet form when describing his unrequited love in Act 1 scene 1 (although, symbolically, he keeps being interrupted).

Key Quotations to Learn

Romeo: '… let lips do what hands do: / They pray …' (Iv)

Romeo: 'How silver-sweet sound lovers' tongues by night, / Like softest music to attending ears.' (IIii)

Juliet: 'Parting is such sweet sorrow / That I shall say good night till it be morrow.' (IIii)

Summary

- Shakespeare conveys true love through religious images and references to lips and hands.
- True love is presented as powerful, impulsive and eternal.
- Family, banishment and rival suitors are all presented as obstacles to love.
- The pain of unrequited love is explored by Shakespeare.

Sample Analysis

Love is presented as a source of anxiety, such as through Juliet's words in Act 2 scene 2, 'O swear not by the moon, th'inconstant moon, / […] Lest that thy love prove likewise variable', when she fears that Romeo's emotions may be fickle. Shakespeare uses the repeated symbol of the moon – and its traditional literary associations with the cycle of time – to convey the idea that Romeo's passion may not last. This is emphasised through the adjectives 'inconstant' and 'variable', as well as the dramatic irony that arises from the audience's awareness that he has only just forsaken Rosaline. Her exclamation 'O swear not' and the word 'lest' show her concerns and her desperation to believe in Romeo's fidelity.

Questions

QUICK TEST
1. When they first meet, what does Romeo compare Juliet with?
2. What does she compare him with in return?
3. How do the deaths of Romeo and Juliet at the end of the play link to true love?
4. What is significant about the way Shakespeare constructs the first shared dialogue between Romeo and Juliet?

EXAM PRACTICE
Using one or more of the 'Key Quotations to Learn', write a paragraph analysing how Shakespeare presents true love.

Conflict

You must be able to: analyse how Shakespeare explores the theme of conflict.

How is conflict presented in a comic manner?

The initial conflict between the Capulet and Montague servants is light-hearted.

In Act 1 scene 1, this is achieved linguistically through Gregory and Sampson's sexual innuendos, such as 'My naked weapon is out'. They also use lots of puns, for example playing with the different meanings of colliers, choler, collar to describe wanting to fight the Montagues despite the punishment for killing someone (being a collier was a popular saying that referred to feeling insulted; choler means anger; collar was another word for a hangman's noose).

Conflict is also achieved structurally, through **stichomythia**: Sampson and Gregory exchange alternating quick-witted responses, with coupling of words (we, draw, quickly moved, moves, stand, wall, weak, men, heads, maids, sense, feel) throughout the first thirty lines to create an energetic rhythm. This continues into the actual dispute with Abraham and Balthasar through the repeated references to thumb-biting and quarrelling.

How is conflict presented as being tragic?

The early comedy makes the later conflicts seem more tragic, particularly the killing of Mercutio but also the deaths of Tybalt and Paris.

All are linked either to mistakes or to sudden and regrettable temper. For example, Romeo accidentally causes his friend's death, '*Tybalt under Romeo's arm thrusts Mercutio in*', while Paris mistakenly thinks Romeo has come to desecrate the Capulet tomb, 'This is that banish'd haughty Montague / [...] come to do some villainous shame / To the dead bodies'. Romeo kills Tybalt in furious revenge and then seems shocked at what he has done, 'Romeo, away, be gone, / The citizens are up, and Tybalt slain! / Stand not amaz'd'.

The responses to these conflicts are more moving, such as Benvolio saying, 'Mercutio is dead, / That gallant spirit hath aspired the clouds', or more impassioned: 'Romeo must not live'.

The consequences are also more immediate and far-reaching, with Romeo's banishment leading directly to his and Juliet's death.

How does Shakespeare present family conflict?

Conflict is also presented within families, particularly in Act 3 scene 5 when Lord Capulet loses his temper with Juliet. There are many insults and even threats of violence, 'My fingers itch'. The conflict is also shown through interruption, with Lady Capulet cutting across her husband's insult of Juliet: 'You tallow face!' / 'Fie, fie. What are you mad?'

Lord Capulet's role in family conflict can also be seen in Act 1 scene 5 where he argues with Tybalt. Here, from Tybalt's point of view, conflict is also linked to protecting family honour, 'Uncle, this is a Montague, our foe: / A villain that is hither come in spite / To scorn at our solemnity this night'.

Key Quotations to Learn

Benvolio: 'And to't they go like lightning: for ere I / Could draw to part them, was stout Tybalt slain.' (IIi)

Lord Capulet: '... go with Paris to Saint Peter's Church, / Or I will drag thee on a hurdle thither.' (IIIv)

Romeo: 'Put not another sin upon my head / By urging me to fury.' (Viii)

Summary

- Conflict is initially presented with a comic aspect.
- Later conflicts, such as the deaths of Mercutio and Tybalt, are much more tragic.
- These later conflicts are more moving and dramatic, with more serious consequences.
- Conflict is also presented between family members and as a means of maintaining family honour.

Sample Analysis

The tragedy of conflict is conveyed by Friar Laurence, 'Alack, alack, what blood is this which stains / The stony entrance of this sepulchre?', when he finds evidence of Romeo and Paris's fight. The verb 'stains' is used literally and metaphorically to suggest how violence is unholy and a dishonour to the surrounding tombs. His sadness and disapproval is emphasised by the **sibilance** and the repetition of the exclamation 'alack'. The sense of tragedy is increased by the Friar's awareness that these events need not have happened and his **guilt** at being partly to blame.

Questions

QUICK TEST
1. What structural technique is used to make Sampson and Gregory's presentation of conflict humorous?
2. In what ways are Mercutio and Paris's deaths linked to accidents?
3. What does Romeo appear to feel immediately after killing Tybalt?
4. With which members of his family does Lord Capulet come into conflict?

EXAM PRACTICE
Using one or more of the 'Key Quotations to Learn', write a paragraph analysing how Shakespeare presents violence at different points in the play.

Inner Turmoil

You must be able to: analyse how Shakespeare explores different types of mental conflict.

How is unrequited love presented?

In the first scene, Romeo compares the chaos of the recent fight with his own turbulent feelings of unrequited love for Rosaline, 'Here's much to do with hate, but more with love. / Why then, O brawling love, O loving hate'. The contrasts, oxymorons and exclamations reflect his troubled mind.

His emotional suffering at not having his love returned is later conveyed through a list of **analogies**: 'bound more than a madman is: / Shut up in prison, kept without food, / Whipp'd and tormented'.

What distress does Juliet experience?

Juliet wrestles with the idea of loving a Montague but her inner turmoil is more dramatic when she discovers that Romeo has killed Tybalt.

Her grief when she believes Romeo has killed himself ('This torture should be roar'd in dismal hell'), turns to shock when she believes he and Tybalt have both died ('Then dreadful trumpet sound the general doom, / For who is living if those two are gone?').

When Juliet finally understands, Shakespeare uses metaphor to show her horror at the idea of loving the murderer of her cousin: 'O serpent heart, hid with a flowering face'.

A series of exclamations and oxymorons develop this clash of love and hate until she begins to defend Romeo and excuse his actions. At this point her inner turmoil focuses on Romeo's exile, with hyperbole emphasising her feeling of desolation, '"Romeo is banished": to speak that word / Is father, mother, Tybalt, Romeo, Juliet, / All slain, all dead'.

Where does anguish provoke suicidal thoughts?

Romeo cannot accept that exile is a better punishment than execution. He says he would rather Friar Laurence had killed him than brought news of Prince Escalus's order, 'Had'st thou no poison mix'd, no sharp-ground knife, / No sudden mean of death, though ne'er so mean, / But "banish'd" to kill me?'

The Friar's line 'Hold thy desperate hand' implies that Romeo prepares to stab himself. He uses a similar phrase in Act 4 scene 1 ('Hold, daughter') when Juliet, holding a knife, announces, 'I long to die / If what thou speak'st speak not of remedy'.

Juliet is faced with the religious crime of marrying another man, 'God join'd my heart and Romeo's, thou our hands', and personification is used to convey her distress at the idea of having to love someone else, 'Or my true heart with treacherous revolt / Turn to another'.

Key Quotations to Learn

Romeo: 'Love is a smoke made with the fume of sighs;' (Ii)

Juliet: 'Was ever book containing such vile matter / So fairly bound? O, that deceit should dwell / In such a gorgeous palace!' (IIIii)

Juliet: 'Come weep with me, past hope, past cure, past help!' (IVi)

Summary

- Romeo displays inner turmoil due to unrequited love and being separated from Juliet.
- Juliet displays inner turmoil at their separation and when she has to confront the fact that Romeo killed her cousin.
- Both are drawn towards suicide by their feelings of distress.
- Shakespeare often uses exclamations, oxymorons, rhetorical questions and metaphors to convey the characters' mental conflict.

Sample Analysis

Inner turmoil can be seen when Romeo makes his way to an apothecary after discovering Juliet's death. Shakespeare uses personification in the phrase, 'O mischief thou art swift / To enter into the thoughts of desperate men' to convey how quickly Romeo's mind turns to suicide. The adjective 'desperate' shows that, without Juliet, he feels he has nothing left. By planning suicide, which would have been considered a mortal sin in the Catholic country of Italy, it is clear that Romeo also feels he is beyond any spiritual hope or guidance.

Questions

QUICK TEST
1. Which event in the play does Romeo compare his unrequited love with?
2. What two things does Juliet mistakenly believe before she finds out that Romeo has killed Tybalt?
3. What can't Romeo accept about the Prince's decree of banishment?
4. What does Friar Laurence have to stop both Romeo and Juliet from doing?

EXAM PRACTICE
Using one or more of the 'Key Quotations to Learn', write a paragraph analysing how Shakespeare presents inner turmoil at different points in the play.

Family Relationships

You must be able to: analyse how Shakespeare explores the theme of family relationships.

Do the Montagues and Capulets display traditional expectations of family?

Both families are presented traditionally, with the man as the head of the house. Lady Capulet is quite strong-willed but she follows her husband's orders, 'Go you to Juliet ere you go to bed, / Prepare her, wife, against this wedding day', and defers to him, 'Here comes your father, tell him so yourself'.

The young men in the families appear to have more freedom than the girls: they are depicted amongst friends in different parts of Verona, whereas Juliet is always shown indoors. This is typical of attitudes to gender in Shakespeare's time.

Although Capulet says Juliet's choice in marriage is important, suitors are expected to go through him. Ultimately, it is his decision, and his fury when she refuses to marry Paris shows how unusual it was for a girl to disobey her father.

How does Shakespeare present loving parent–child relationships?

Lord and Lady Capulet care about Juliet. Her father appears particularly protective, such as when he sympathises with her sadness by comparing her to a fountain, 'How now, a conduit, girl?'

Similarly, Lady Montague worries about her son, 'Right glad I am he was not at this fray', and Lord Montague wishes he could make Romeo happier, 'Could we but learn from whence his sorrows grow, / We would as willingly give cure as know'.

In the final scene, Lord Montague explains the cause of his wife's death as, 'Grief of my son's exile hath stopped her breath'. Likewise, Lady Capulet says she feels near to dying when she sees Juliet's dead body, 'This sight of death is as a bell / That warns my old age to a sepulchre'.

Where does Shakespeare present problems between children and parents?

The distance between parent and child is shown by Shakespeare's inclusion of go-betweens. Juliet has had a nurse since she was born, being breast-fed by her rather than by her own mother. The Montagues ask Benvolio for help when they can't get through to Romeo, but their son actually confides more in the Friar. However, this distance (especially the presence of a nurse) was usual for wealthier families in the time Shakespeare was writing.

The parents are also presented as setting a bad example. As well as the overall feud, Lord Capulet is hot-headed and aggressive (although he berates Tybalt for the same behaviour) and his wife pushes Juliet towards an early marriage because, 'Younger than you / Here in Verona, ladies of esteem, / Are made already mothers'.

Key Quotations to Learn

Lord Montague [about Romeo]: 'But to himself so secret and so close, / So far from sounding and discovery,' (Ii)

Lady Capulet: 'The County Paris, at Saint Peter's Church, / Shall happily make thee there a joyful bride.' (IIIv)

Lord Capulet: '... Wife, we scarce thought us blest, / That God had lent us but this only child; / But now I see this one is one too much / And that we have a curse in having her:' (IIIv)

Summary

- The Montagues and Capulets are presented as traditional, patriarchal families.
- The parents love their children and worry about them.
- However, they are also distanced from their children, with Benvolio and the Nurse playing the roles of go-betweens.
- The parents set a bad example to their children, particularly in terms of the Montague–Capulet feud.

Sample Analysis

Despite Capulet's behaviour in Act 3 scene 5, we see his true feelings for Juliet after she is found apparently dead. In the lines, 'Death is my son-in-law, Death is my heir. / My daughter he hath wedded. I will die, / And leave him all: life, living, all is Death's', repeated personification conveys the depth of his grief. The certainty of the modal verb in 'I will die' also shows how much her death has affected him. The image of death being his 'heir' reflects the fact that Juliet was his only child, as well as the desolation he feels at losing her. This despair is emphasised by the pattern of three that ends the quotation, suggesting he feels he has nothing left in the world.

Questions

QUICK TEST
1. Who seems more dominant, Lord or Lady Capulet?
2. In what ways are boys and girls treated differently by their families?
3. What happens to Lady Montague at the end of the play?
4. In what ways do the Montagues and Capulets appear to set a bad example to their children?

EXAM PRACTICE
Using one or more of the 'Key Quotations to Learn', write a paragraph analysing how Shakespeare presents family relationships in the play.

Fate

You must be able to: analyse how Shakespeare explores the theme of fate.

What is fate?

Fate, or destiny, is the idea that one's life is predetermined by some supernatural or spiritual power. This was a widespread belief when Shakespeare was writing; astrology, the theory that the stars can reveal the future, was part of this and is still popular today.

Romeo and Juliet are fated to die and Shakespeare builds up a sense that they cannot avoid the chain of events leading to their suicides.

How does Shakespeare make Romeo and Juliet's fate clear?

Shakespeare establishes the theme of fate in the Prologue. The fifth line says, 'From forth the fatal loins of these two foes', meaning that when Romeo and Juliet are born their destinies are already decided. They are described as 'star-cross'd' and 'death-mark'd', suggesting some higher power has predetermined their lives and deaths.

Revealing the play's ending reinforces the idea of fate and emphasises the atmosphere of tragedy, as the audience watch knowing that nothing can change the outcome.

Where do Romeo and Juliet see themselves as unlucky?

There are many references to fortune, or luck. After killing Tybalt, Romeo exclaims, 'O, I am fortune's fool', and Juliet later says, 'O Fortune, Fortune! All men call thee fickle'.

Fortune is personified as a higher power, controlling the lives of the two lovers. The word 'fool' suggests that Fortune brings Romeo bad luck and laughs at him, while 'fickle' depicts fortune as unpredictable: it has brought them together but is now driving them apart.

How does Shakespeare include prophecies of disaster?

Romeo and Juliet have several visions of death that foreshadow the events of Act 5 scene 3.

When Romeo leaves Juliet to begin his exile, she says to him 'thou look'st pale' and ominously compares him to a corpse in a tomb. Before being brought news of Juliet's apparent death, Romeo describes how, 'I dreamt my lady came and found me dead'.

Many other lines foreshadow their fate, such as when Juliet drinks the sleeping potion and pledges, 'Romeo, Romeo, Romeo, here's drink! I drink to thee!', creating a clear parallel with Romeo's suicide by poison.

Juliet also mentions different **classical gods**, reinforcing the idea that her life is being manipulated by some higher power. While waiting for Romeo in Act 3 scene 2, she refers to Phaeton – the son of the Greek god Helios – whose recklessness led him to be killed by the god Zeus. This foretells Romeo's death and mirrors his banishment by Prince Escalus.

Shakespeare also includes lots of prophetic death imagery, such as Mercutio's joke about unrequited love: 'Alas poor Romeo, he is already dead'.

Key Quotations to Learn

Juliet: 'O God, I have an ill-divining soul! / Methinks I see thee, now thou art so low, / As one dead in the bottom of a tomb.' (IIIv)

Romeo: 'Then I defy you, stars!' (Vi)

Romeo [about Paris]: 'One writ with me in sour misfortune's book.' (Viii)

Summary

- Fate is the idea that our lives have been predetermined by some supernatural force. Fate was a popular belief in Shakespeare's time.
- The Prologue establishes that Romeo and Juliet are fated to kill themselves.
- Fortune, or luck, is personified to present the characters as being manipulated by higher powers.
- Shakespeare uses visions, death imagery and classical references to foreshadow Romeo and Juliet's ultimate fate.

Sample Analysis

The notion that Romeo and Juliet are fated to die is emphasised in Act 3 scene 5 after their wedding night. When Romeo describes the night as, 'The vaulty heaven so high above our heads', Shakespeare also creates an image of the gods looking down on the two lovers. Romeo uses the adjective 'vaulty' to convey the scale of the night sky but Shakespeare is also foreshadowing Romeo and Juliet's suicide in the Capulet vault. Dramatic irony is created two lines later when Romeo flippantly declares, 'Come death, and welcome', as the audience have been aware since the Prologue that both characters will die.

Questions

QUICK TEST
1. Why might Shakespeare have revealed the outcome of the play at the very start?
2. What does Romeo feel about fortune, or the gods, after he has killed Tybalt?
3. How does Shakespeare foreshadow Romeo's suicide by poison?
4. What ominous vision does Romeo have in Act 5?

EXAM PRACTICE
Using one or more of the 'Key Quotations to Learn', write a paragraph analysing how Shakespeare presents fate in the play.

You must be able to: analyse how Shakespeare uses and explores ideas about time.

How does time affect the narrative of the play?

The story takes place over only four days, adding an urgent intensity to Romeo and Juliet's love. This speed links to the theme of fate, as if events are out of their control, which Shakespeare develops with **coincidence** and mistiming. He highlights this speed to the audience through the Prologue, 'The two hours' traffic of our stage'.

How are characters rushed by others?

Shakespeare presents characters being rushed, creating a sense that they are not in control of their destinies.

Paris urges Lord Capulet to allow him to marry Juliet, and she is rushed by Lady Capulet.

Benvolio hurries Romeo to the feast and he has a feeling of **foreboding**; Shakespeare implies that if the timings had been different, Romeo and Juliet might never have met.

Juliet rushes the Nurse for Romeo's message and, on her wedding night, uses classical imagery, 'Gallop apace you fiery-footed steeds' to convey her wish that time would speed up.

Lord Capulet organises Juliet's wedding for three days' time. The metaphor, 'I'll have this knot knit up tomorrow morning', later reveals his intention to advance the wedding.

Which characters meet an untimely end?

Shakespeare repeatedly uses 'untimely' to describe the many early deaths in the play.

Benvolio says Mercutio 'too untimely here did scorn the earth' and this is quickly followed by Tybalt's death.

When Juliet fakes her death, Lord Capulet laments, 'Death lies on her like an untimely frost'. Using a rhetorical question and repetition to convey his shock, he also personifies time as a cruel killer: 'time, why cam'st thou now / To murder, murder our solemnity?'

Her actual death is preceded by those of Paris and Romeo, 'here untimely lay / The noble Paris and true Romeo dead'. The audience are also told of Lady Montague's sudden death.

Where else is untimeliness presented by Shakespeare?

Shakespeare makes different events happen at the wrong time. This is most obvious when Friar Laurence's letter misses Romeo, leading him to kill himself before Juliet awakes. Tragic irony arises from her fear, before taking the sleeping potion, that the timing would be wrong and she would wake too early, 'How if, when I am laid into the tomb, / I wake before the time that Romeo / Come to redeem me?'

The Friar has hopes that different circumstances will arise when their marriage can be revealed, 'till we can find a time / To blaze your marriage', while Lady Capulet cannot see that the marriage to Paris is bad timing: 'a sudden day of joy'.

Key Quotations to Learn

Romeo: 'Some consequence yet hanging in the stars / Shall bitterly begin his fearful date / With this night's revels and expire the term / Of a despised life closed in my breast / By some vile forfeit of untimely death.' (Iiv)

Friar Laurence: 'Ah what an unkind hour / Is guilty of this lamentable chance?' (Viii)

Friar Laurence: '... their stol'n marriage-day / Was Tybalt's doomsday, whose untimely death / Banish'd the new-made bridegroom from the city,' (Viii)

Summary

- The short time-frame of the play intensifies Romeo and Juliet's love.
- It also creates a sense that events are out of the characters' control.
- Shakespeare emphasises this by having characters rushed by others, including untimely deaths, and creating coincidence and mistiming.

Sample Analysis

Having established Romeo and Juliet's deaths in the Prologue, Shakespeare regularly creates dramatic irony around the issue of time. Leaving for Mantua, Romeo promises Juliet, 'I doubt it not; and all these woes shall serve / For sweet discourses in our time to come', and the modal verb 'shall' shows his certainty that they have a future together. This reference to a future that the audience know will not happen increases the sense of tragedy within the scene. The play is full of images of duality and the contrast of 'woes' and 'sweet discourses' is significant as the two lovers will never actually achieve happiness.

Questions

QUICK TEST
1. How many days is the story of the play set across?
2. Which characters die early?
3. How are Romeo and Juliet's deaths linked to different mistimings?
4. What other major theme of the play does Shakespeare link to time?

EXAM PRACTICE
Using one or more of the 'Key Quotations to Learn', write a paragraph analysing how Shakespeare presents the significance of time at different points in the play.

Tips and Assessment Objectives

You must be able to: understand how to approach the exam question and meet the requirements of the mark scheme.

Quick tips

- You will get one question divided into two parts. Part A will ask you to analyse a short extract from the play and will usually be focussed on character. Part B will usually focus on a specific theme, asking you to explore how it is shown in other parts of the play and how it relates to context.

- Make sure you know what the question is asking you. Underline key words and pay particular attention to the bullet point prompts that come with the question.

- You should spend about 55 minutes on your *Romeo and Juliet* response, dividing your time equally between the two parts of the question. Allow yourself between five and ten minutes to annotate the extract and plan your answer so there is some structure to your essay.

- It can sometimes help, after each paragraph, to quickly re-read the question to keep yourself focussed on the exam task.

- Keep your writing concise. If you waste time 'waffling' you won't be able to include the full range of skills that the mark scheme requires.

- It is a good idea to remember what the mark scheme is asking of you ...

Part A

AO2: Analyse effects of Shakespeare's language, form and structure (20 marks)

You need to comment on how specific words, language techniques, sentence structures, stage directions, or the narrative structure allow Shakespeare to get his ideas across to the audience.

Lower	Middle	Upper
Identification of some different methods used by Shakespeare to convey meaning. Some subject terminology.	Explanation of Shakespeare's different methods. Clear understanding of the effects of these methods. Accurate use of subject terminology.	Analysis of the full range of Shakespeare's methods. Thorough exploration of the effects of these methods. Accurate range of subject terminology.

Part B

AO1: Understand and respond to the play (15 marks)

This is all about coming up with a range of points that match the question, interpreting and explaining Shakespeare's ideas, supporting these ideas with references from the play and writing your essay in a mature, academic style.

Lower	Middle	Upper
The essay has some good ideas that are mostly relevant. Some quotations and references are used to support ideas.	A clear essay that always focusses on the exam question. Quotations and references support ideas effectively. The response refers to different points in the play.	A convincing, well-structured essay that answers the question fully. Quotations and references are well-chosen and integrated into sentences. The response covers the whole play (not everything, but ideas from a range of Acts).

AO3: Understand the relationship between the play and its contexts (5 marks)

For this part of the mark scheme, you need to show your understanding of how the characters or Shakespeare's ideas relate to when he was writing (1590s) or the play's setting (fourteenth-century Italy).

Lower	Middle	Upper
Some awareness of how ideas in the play link to its context.	References to relevant aspects of context show a clear understanding.	Specific aspects of the play's contexts are integrated with interpretations to show a detailed understanding.

Romeo and Juliet: Act 1 scene 5, lines 92–111

In this extract, Romeo and Juliet meet for the first time.

ROMEO	If I profane with my unworthiest hand This holy shrine, the gentle fine is this: My lips, two blushing pilgrims, ready stand To smooth that rough touch with a tender kiss.
JULIET	Good pilgrim, you do wrong your hand too much, Which mannerly devotion shows in this; For saints have hands that pilgrims' hands do touch, And palm to palm is holy palmers' kiss.
ROMEO	Have not saints lips, and holy palmers too?
JULIET	Ay, pilgrim, lips that they must use in prayer.
ROMEO	O, then, dear saint, let lips do what hands do; They pray, grant thou, lest faith turn to despair.
JULIET	Saints do not move, though grant for prayers' sake.
ROMEO	Then move not, while my prayer's effect I take. Thus from my lips, by yours, my sin is purged.
JULIET	Then have my lips the sin that they have took.
ROMEO	Sin from thy lips? O trespass sweetly urged! Give me my sin again.
JULIET	You kiss by the book.
NURSE	Madam, your mother craves a word with you.
ROMEO	What is her mother?
NURSE	Marry, bachelor, Her mother is the lady of the house.

1. a. Explore how Shakespeare, in this extract, presents the relationship between Romeo and Juliet. Refer closely to the extract in your answer.   [20 marks]

   b. In this extract, Romeo and Juliet meet and fall in love, unaware that they come from rival families. Explain the importance of love elsewhere in the play.

   In your answer, you must consider:

   • how love is shown   • the effects of love in the play.

   You must refer to the context of the play in your answer.   [20 marks]

Romeo and Juliet: Act 5 scene 3, lines 74–105

In this extract, Romeo has just killed Paris and then enters Juliet's tomb.

> ROMEO   Let me peruse this face.
> Mercutio's kinsman, noble County Paris!
> What said my man, when my betossed soul
> Did not attend him as we rode? I think
> He told me Paris should have married Juliet:
> Said he not so? or did I dream it so?
> Or am I mad, hearing him talk of Juliet,
> To think it was so? O, give me thy hand,
> One writ with me in sour misfortune's book!
> I'll bury thee in a triumphant grave;
> A grave? O no! a lantern, slaughter'd youth,
> For here lies Juliet, and her beauty makes
> This vault a feasting presence full of light.
> Death, lie thou there, by a dead man interr'd.
>
> *[Laying PARIS in the tomb]*
>
>   How oft when men are at the point of death
> Have they been merry! which their keepers call
> A lightning before death: O, how may I
> Call this a lightning? O my love! my wife!
> Death, that hath suck'd the honey of thy breath,
> Hath had no power yet upon thy beauty:
> Thou art not conquer'd; beauty's ensign yet
> Is crimson in thy lips and in thy cheeks,
> And death's pale flag is not advanced there.
> Tybalt, liest thou there in thy bloody sheet?
> O, what more favour can I do to thee,
> Than with that hand that cut thy youth in twain
> To sunder his that was thine enemy?
> Forgive me, cousin! Ah, dear Juliet,
> Why art thou yet so fair? shall I believe
> That unsubstantial death is amorous,
> And that the lean abhorred monster keeps
> Thee here in dark to be his paramour?

2. a. Explore how Shakespeare, in this extract, presents Romeo. Refer closely
to the extract in your answer. [20 marks]

   b. In this extract, Shakespeare shows Romeo's belief that he and Paris are victims of
fate. Explain the importance of fate elsewhere in the play.

     In your answer, you must consider:

     • how fate is shown   • why fate is important in the play.

     You must refer to the context of the play in your answer. [20 marks]

Possible Questions

Romeo and Juliet: Act 1 scene 1, lines 58–80

In this extract, an argument between a Montague servant (Abraham) and a Capulet servant (Sampson) turns into a fight between the two families.

ABRAHAM	You lie.
SAMPSON	Draw, if you be men. Gregory, remember thy swashing blow.
[They fight. Enter BENVOLIO]	
BENVOLIO	Part, fools! Put up your swords; you know not what you do.
[Beats down their swords. Enter TYBALT]	
TYBALT	What, art thou drawn among these heartless hinds? Turn thee, Benvolio, look upon thy death.
BENVOLIO	I do but keep the peace: put up thy sword, Or manage it to part these men with me.
TYBALT	What, drawn, and talk of peace! I hate the word, As I hate hell, all Montagues, and thee: Have at thee, coward!
[They fight. Enter, several of both houses, who join the fray; then enter Citizens, with clubs]	
FIRST CITIZEN	Clubs, bills, and partisans! strike! beat them down! Down with the Capulets! down with the Montagues!
[Enter CAPULET in his gown, and LADY CAPULET]	
CAPULET	What noise is this? Give me my long sword, ho!
LADY CAPULET	A crutch, a crutch! why call you for a sword?
CAPULET	My sword, I say! Old Montague is come, And flourishes his blade in spite of me.
[Enter MONTAGUE and LADY MONTAGUE]	
MONTAGUE	Thou villain Capulet, – Hold me not, let me go.
LADY MONTAGUE	Thou shalt not stir a foot to seek a foe.
[Enter PRINCE, with Attendants]	
PRINCE	Rebellious subjects, enemies to peace, Profaners of this neighbour-stained steel,–

3. a. Explore how Shakespeare, in this extract, presents the relationship between the two families. Refer closely to the extract in your answer.   **[20 marks]**

   b. In this extract, Shakespeare shows the conflict between the two families. Explain the importance of conflict elsewhere in the play.

   In your answer, you must consider:

   • how conflict is shown   • the effects of conflict in the play.

   You must refer to the context of the play in your answer.   **[20 marks]**

Romeo and Juliet: Act 4 scene 3, lines 24–50

In this extract, Juliet prepares to take the sleeping potion that the Friar has given her to fake her death.

JULIET   What if it be a poison, which the friar
Subtly hath minister'd to have me dead,
Lest in this marriage he should be dishonour'd,
Because he married me before to Romeo?
I fear it is: and yet, methinks, it should not,
For he hath still been tried a holy man.
How if, when I am laid into the tomb,
I wake before the time that Romeo
Come to redeem me? there's a fearful point!
Shall I not, then, be stifled in the vault,
To whose foul mouth no healthsome air breathes in,
And there die strangled ere my Romeo comes?
Or, if I live, is it not very like,
The horrible conceit of death and night,
Together with the terror of the place,–
As in a vault, an ancient receptacle,
Where, for these many hundred years, the bones
Of all my buried ancestors are packed:
Where bloody Tybalt, yet but green in earth,
Lies festering in his shroud; where, as they say,
At some hours in the night spirits resort;–
Alack, alack, is it not like that I,
So early waking, what with loathsome smells,
And shrieks like mandrakes' torn out of the earth,
That living mortals, hearing them, run mad:–
O, if I wake, shall I not be distraught,
Environed with all these hideous fears?

4. a. Explore how Shakespeare, in this extract, presents Juliet.

      Refer closely to the extract in your answer.   **[20 marks]**

  b. In this extract, Shakespeare presents Juliet in a state of anguish or emotional pain. Explain the importance of anguish elsewhere in the play.

      In your answer, you must consider:

      • how anguish is shown   • the effects of anguish in the play.

      You must refer to the context of the play in your answer.   **[20 marks]**

Planning a Response to the Exam Question

You must be able to: understand what an exam question is asking and prepare your response.

A typical question will look like this:

Romeo and Juliet: Act 1 scene 2, lines 1–34

In this extract, Lord Capulet and Paris discuss the feud with the Montagues, and Paris's wish to marry Juliet.

CAPULET	But Montague is bound as well as I, In penalty alike; and 'tis not hard, I think, For men so old as we to keep the peace.
PARIS	Of honourable reckoning are you both; And pity 'tis you lived at odds so long. But now, my lord, what say you to my suit?
CAPULET	But saying o'er what I have said before: My child is yet a stranger in the world; She hath not seen the change of fourteen years, Let two more summers wither in their pride, Ere we may think her ripe to be a bride.
PARIS	Younger than she are happy mothers made.
CAPULET	And too soon marr'd are those so early made. The earth hath swallow'd all my hopes but she, She is the hopeful lady of my earth: But woo her, gentle Paris, get her heart, My will to her consent is but a part; An she agree, within her scope of choice Lies my consent and fair according voice. This night I hold an old accustom'd feast, Whereto I have invited many a guest, Such as I love; and you, among the store, One more, most welcome, makes my number more. At my poor house look to behold this night Earth-treading stars that make dark heaven light: Such comfort as do lusty young men feel When well-apparell'd April on the heel Of limping winter treads, even such delight Among fresh female buds shall you this night Inherit at my house; hear all, all see, And like her most whose merit most shall be: Which on more view, of many mine being one May stand in number, though in reckoning none, Come, go with me.

1. a. Explore how Shakespeare, in this extract, presents Lord Capulet.

Refer closely to the extract in your answer. [20 marks]

b. In this extract, Shakespeare shows Lord Capulet's thoughts about his daughter, Juliet. Explain the importance of parent–child relationships elsewhere in the play.

In your answer, you must consider:
* how parent–child relationships are shown
* the effects of parent–child relationships in the play.

You must refer to the context of the play in your answer. [20 marks]

How do I work out what to do?

The question is in two parts and each has a different, but linked, focus. In Part A the focus is Lord Capulet in the extract; in Part B the focus is parent–child relationships elsewhere in the play.

If you are unsure how to approach Part A, the focus of Part B gives you a hint: you should analyse how Lord Capulet is presented as a parent and his feelings about Juliet.

How do I prepare to answer Part A?

You need to focus only on the extract. What does it show you about Lord Capulet and how is this conveyed? 'How' is the key aspect of this question.

You are only being assessed for AO2, so you need to analyse the different ways in which Shakespeare's use of language, structure and form help to show the audience what Lord Capulet is like. All of your ideas should be related to specific quotations from the extract.

Do not include references to context in Part A because you will not receive any marks for them.

How do I work with the extract?

Read the question first then read the extract all the way through. After that, re-read the extract, highlighting or underlining key quotations that show what Lord Capulet is like.

You only have about 25 minutes to write your answer. Don't try to annotate the whole extract. Just try to select three or four of the most useful quotations: ideally ones that include different features of language, structure and form so your analysis is varied.

You can then turn each of your quotations into a concise paragraph of analysis. Your idea doesn't have to be different each time. For example, you might write three paragraphs analysing how Lord Capulet feels about Juliet, followed by two paragraphs analysing how he comes across as the head of the Capulet family.

Where possible, try to develop your analysis with a link to another part of the extract, especially if it gives you the chance to explore another feature of Shakespeare's writing.

Planning a Response to the Exam Question

How do I prepare to answer Part B?

For Part B, you need to use relevant quotations that you have learned from elsewhere in the play. 'Explain' and 'importance' are key aspects of this question.

For AO1, you need to display a clear understanding of where parent–child relationships are an important part of the play, and what effect they have on characters and events. Your ideas need to be well-structured, clearly expressed and supported by evidence.

For AO3, you need to link your explanation to the play's context, considering how it affects the way parent–child relationships are presented.

Do not include detailed AO2 analysis in Part B because you will not receive any marks for it.

How can I plan my response?

You have approximately 25 minutes to write this part of your answer. This isn't long but spend a few minutes writing a quick plan. This will help you to focus your thoughts and produce a well-structured essay.

Try to come up with three or four ideas based on the quotations that you have learned. Think of different parts of the play rather than focussing on one scene. Each idea can then be written up as a paragraph.

Plan in whatever way you find most useful.

Students have found the following planning formats useful:

- List
- Two-column table (AO1 ideas one side; AO3 context the other side)
- Flow diagram
- Tree mind map (with branches for AO1 and AO3 ideas)

Spider diagrams are particularly popular; they provide a clear way to organise and then order your ideas. Look at the example on the opposite page where the student has come up with four areas to focus on. For each area, there is an AO1 idea, a reference to AO3 context, and the quotation that they will use as evidence.

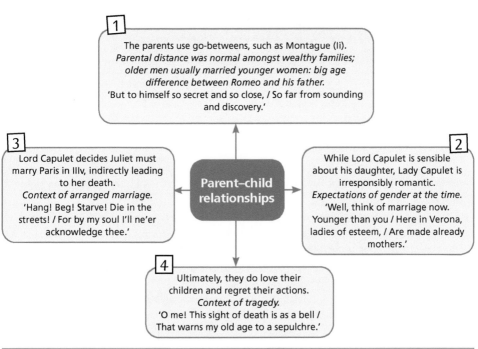

1
The parents use go-betweens, such as Montague (Ii).
Parental distance was normal amongst wealthy families; older men usually married younger women: big age difference between Romeo and his father.
'But to himself so secret and so close, / So far from sounding and discovery.'

3
Lord Capulet decides Juliet must marry Paris in IIIv, indirectly leading to her death.
Context of arranged marriage.
'Hang! Beg! Starve! Die in the streets! / For by my soul I'll ne'er acknowledge thee.'

Parent–child relationships

2
While Lord Capulet is sensible about his daughter, Lady Capulet is irresponsibly romantic.
Expectations of gender at the time.
'Well, think of marriage now. Younger than you / Here in Verona, ladies of esteem, / Are made already mothers.'

4
Ultimately, they do love their children and regret their actions.
Context of tragedy.
'O me! This sight of death is as a bell / That warns my old age to a sepulchre.'

Summary

- Make sure you know what the focus of the essay is.
- In Part A, remember to analyse how ideas are conveyed by Shakespeare.
- In Part B, explain your ideas and relate them to the play's context.

Questions

QUICK TEST
1. What key skills do you need to show in Part A of your response?
2. What key skills do you need to show in Part B of your response?
3. What are the benefits of quickly planning your response to Part B?

EXAM PRACTICE
Prepare and plan a response to Question 1 from page 58.

Grade 5 Annotated Response to Part A

1. a. Explore how Shakespeare, in this extract, presents Lord Capulet. Refer closely to the extract in your answer.

[20 marks]

In the extract from Act 1 scene 2, Shakespeare presents what Lord Capulet is like as a man and as a father [1].

Lord Capulet doesn't want Paris to marry Juliet yet because she is only thirteen. 'Let two more summers wither in their pride, / Ere we may think her ripe to be a bride'. This shows he is protective of his daughter and thinks she is too young for marriage [2]. Although Paris tries to persuade him on line 12, Capulet isn't put off and says that early marriages often end up as unhappy marriages. This shows he cares for Juliet's happiness [3].

As well as wanting to be sure that Juliet is happy, Capulet also appears quite romantic. 'Woo her, gentle Paris, get her heart'. This focuses on true love. The verb 'woo' suggests he should court her in the traditional romantic way in order to win her love [4]. Capulet also tests Paris's love by inviting him to the feast and encouraging him to look at other girls to make sure Juliet is the one that he wants, 'delight / Among fresh female buds'. This is a metaphor [5].

Shakespeare also links Lord Capulet to tragedy. 'Earth hath swallow'd all my hopes but she'. This is an example of personification and it describes how all his other kids have been buried. It sounds really horrible which makes it sound like their deaths are still really painful to him. He sounds unhappy because he is hopeless [6]. This explains why he's so protective of Juliet as all his other kids are dead so she's all he has left [7].

Capulet is also respectful of Juliet as an individual. 'My will to her consent is but a part'. When the play was set, wealthy fathers often arranged their daughters' marriage and chose a suitable man. Lord Capulet is almost breaking with traditional expectations because he actually says that Juliet's choice is more important than his own. This would have been quite unusual for the time so this suggests Capulet is extra loving of his daughter [8].

1. Basic introduction that could be more focussed and specific. AO2
2. There is a clear point and evidence, although the quotation could be integrated into the sentence. There is some explanation but it requires more specific analysis of language and use of subject terminology. AO2
3. Some attempt is made to develop the paragraph but there isn't a quotation or any specific analysis. AO2
4. A new point is established with clear evidence and analysis of language. The quotation could be embedded. Some subject terminology but a wider range could be used. AO2
5. There is another attempt to develop the paragraph by exploring another quotation. However, this is feature spotting rather than specific analysis. AO2
6. Although expression could be more sophisticated, there is a good point, a well-chosen quotation, clear analysis and some subject terminology. AO2
7. A brief attempt to develop the paragraph would benefit from a specific quotation and analysis. AO2
8. There is a clear point and a well-chosen quotation. However, instead of analysis, much of the paragraph is taken up with references to social context (for which there are no marks in this part of the question). AO2

Questions

EXAM PRACTICE
Choose a paragraph of this essay. Read it through a few times then try to rewrite and improve it. You might:
- Improve the sophistication of the language or the clarity of expression.
- Replace a reference with a quotation or use a better quotation.
- Ensure quotations are embedded in the sentence.
- Provide more detailed, or a wider range of, analysis.
- Use more subject terminology.

1. b. In this extract, Shakespeare shows Lord Capulet's thoughts about his daughter, Juliet. Explain the importance of parent–child relationships elsewhere in the play.

   In your answer, you must consider:

   • how parent–child relationships are shown

   • the effects of parent–child relationships in the play.   [20 marks]

Parent–child relationships are important in Romeo and Juliet. This can be seen in Lord and Lady Capulet and Juliet, and in Lord and Lady Montague and Romeo [1].

In the play, parents struggle to communicate fully with their children. 'to himself so secret and so close, / So far from sounding and discovery'. This is Lord Montague explaining how he cannot help or understand Romeo. Instead he asks Benvolio to talk to Romeo and this shows a gap in communication between parent and child. It was normal in those days for there to be a go-between [2]. Many of the problems in the play arise from the secrets that the youngsters keep due to this lack of communication, such as Romeo and Juliet's love and marriage [3].

Lord and Lady Capulet are both presented as bad parents. This can be seen early in the play where Lady Capulet presents a false view of love as if it's all perfect. She's trying to push her daughter into an early marriage which isn't good parenting. 'Well, think of marriage now. Younger than you / Here in Verona, ladies of esteem, / Are made already mothers'. This matches traditional expectations of marriage because children would get married young [4].

At first, Lord Capulet seems a responsible parent but by Act 3 scene 5 it's obvious that he's really horrible. Instead of being nice to his daughter, he calls her names and says bad things will happen to her. This is because in those days it was the father's choice who the daughter married so he is making that choice for her and doesn't like that she won't go through with it, 'hang! Beg! Starve! Die in the streets! / For by my soul I'll ne'er acknowledge thee', and this links to the tradition of arranged marriages. When you think about it, if Lord Capulet had not said he was going to force Juliet to get married, she would never have taken the sleeping potion and therefore probably wouldn't have ended up dead [5].

At the end of the play, the Montagues and the Capulets do love their children and regret their actions. Montague announces that his wife has died of grief over Romeo's exile and Lady Capulet also says that she's going to die [6]. Both fathers are really unhappy but their grief brings the feud to an end because they know it's their fault so Shakespeare creates a happy ending that is linked to parent–child relationships [7].

1. Basic introduction that could be more focussed and specific. AO1

2. A clear opening point with a well-chosen quotation that could be integrated into the sentence. Social context is relevant but bolted on rather than fully integrated. AO1/AO3

3. There is some attempt to explain the effects of parent–child relationships. AO1

4. The new point expands the range of the essay. There is a well-chosen quotation but it could be integrated. There is relevant social context but this could also be more effectively integrated. AO1/AO3

5. The new point builds on the previous idea. A well-chosen quotation is partly integrated, as is social context, and there is consideration of the effect of parent–child relationships. Expression could be a lot more concise and sophisticated. AO1/AO3

6. The final paragraph expands the range of the essay a little further but lacks a quotation and context. AO1/AO3

7. The final sentence brings the essay to a satisfactory close by attempting to consider the ultimate effect of parent–child relationships. AO1

Questions

EXAM PRACTICE

Choose a paragraph from this essay. Read it through a few times then try to rewrite and improve it. You might:

- Improve the sophistication of the language or the clarity of expression.
- Replace a reference with a quotation or use a better quotation.
- Ensure quotations are embedded in the sentence.
- Provide a clearer interpretation of what is being suggested about parent–child relationships.
- Link some context to the analysis more effectively.

Grade 7+ Annotated Response to Part A

A proportion of the best top-band answers will be awarded Grade 8 or Grade 9. To achieve this, you should aim for a sophisticated, fluent and nuanced response that displays flair and originality.

1. a. Explore how Shakespeare, in this extract, presents Lord Capulet.

   Refer closely to the extract in your answer.

   [20 marks]

In the extract from Act 1 scene 2, Shakespeare presents Lord Capulet as a caring and protective father whose life has been tainted by tragedy [1].

Despite Paris's social status, Lord Capulet is reluctant to let him marry Juliet because she is only thirteen. His suggestion, 'Let two more summers wither in their pride, / Ere we may think her ripe to be a bride', uses nature imagery to assert that Juliet is too young for marriage, and shows his protective attitude [2]. When Paris tries to persuade him on line 12, Capulet is resolute and appears to interrupt him, 'And too soon marr'd are those so early made', repeating Paris's language ('made') and using an internal half-rhyme ('marr'd), to emphasise his fears of an unhappy marriage [3].

As well as wanting to be sure that Juliet is happy, Capulet also appears quite romantic. When he says, 'Woo her, gentle Paris, get her heart', the metaphor focuses on true love. The verb 'woo' and the adjective 'gentle' suggest he is encouraging a slow and tender courtship [4]. Capulet is also quite cunning and appears to want to test Paris's love, inviting him to the feast and encouraging him to look at other girls and make sure Juliet is his desire. The metaphor, 'delight / Among fresh female buds', uses alliteration to heighten a sense of temptation [5].

Shakespeare also adds a sense of tragedy to Lord Capulet. His line, 'The earth hath swallow'd all my hopes but she', uses personification to convey how all his other children have died. The harsh verb 'swallow'd' implies their deaths were very painful to him and the abstract noun 'hopes' emphasises this by suggesting that he is almost devoid of faith and optimism [6]. This helps to explain his protection of Juliet as the phrase, 'She is the hopeful lady of my earth', shows that all his wishes focus on her having a good life. The pronoun in 'my earth' also indicates that his life revolves around her [7].

Perhaps because of this, Capulet also seems respectful of Juliet as an individual. Despite his ability to arrange the marriage, he states, 'My will to her consent is but a part', showing his wish that Juliet should make her own choice of who she marries. The use of the adverb 'but' places his wishes below those of his daughter, again highlighting his love and care of Juliet [8].

1. Clear overview of Lord Capulet to set up the analysis. AO2
2. Clear use of point, evidence and analysis to explore Lord Capulet's character. AO2
3. The point is developed further through another brief quotation and further analysis. There is sophisticated consideration of language, structure and form. AO2
4. A new point is established, supported by evidence and analysis of language and structure. Accurate range of subject terminology. AO2
5. The paragraph is developed through analysis of quite subtle features. AO2
6. A new point adds greater range to the exploration of Capulet. Well-chosen evidence is followed by thoughtful analysis of language. AO2
7. The paragraph is developed through further analysis of language. AO2
8. The final paragraph continues the clear analysis and includes a brief conclusion to draw the response to a close. AO2

Questions

EXAM PRACTICE
Spend 25 minutes writing an answer to Question 1a from page 58.
Remember to make use of the preparation you have already undertaken.

Grade 7+ Annotated Response to Part B

A proportion of the best top-band answers will be awarded Grade 8 or Grade 9. To achieve this, you should aim for a sophisticated, fluent and nuanced response that displays flair and originality.

1. b. In this extract, Shakespeare shows Lord Capulet's thoughts about his daughter, Juliet. Explain the importance of parent–child relationships elsewhere in the play.

   In your answer, you must consider:

   • how parent–child relationships are shown
   • the effects of parent–child relationships in the play. [20 marks]

Parent–child relationships in Romeo and Juliet are shown to be loving yet flawed, leading to the death of the children and the grief of the parents [1].

It is clear that both Montague and Capulet parents struggle to communicate fully with their children. Parental distance was normal amongst wealthy families in the fourteenth century and both families use go-betweens to speak to their children, such as the Nurse and Benvolio. Discussing his son with Benvolio, Lord Montague refers to Romeo as, 'to himself so secret and so close, / So far from sounding and discovery', showing that he cannot help or understand his son [2]. This may also link to the traditional expectations of marriage at the time, with wealthy older men marrying much younger women, possibly leading to an insurmountable age gap between Romeo and his father. Many of the problems in the play arise from the secrets that the youngsters keep due to this lack of communication, such as Romeo and Juliet's marriage [3].

Lord and Lady Capulet are both presented as bad, irresponsible parents. This can be seen early in the play where Lady Capulet presents a falsely idealistic view of love to push her daughter into an early marriage. Her comment, 'Well, think of marriage now. Younger than you / Here in Verona, ladies of esteem, / Are made already mothers', follows traditional expectations of gender for the time the play is set and when it was written [4]. However, Shakespeare makes Juliet particularly young (thirteen) to emphasise her mother's poor sense of judgement. It is perhaps partly Lady Capulet's idealism that moves Juliet to enter into her unwise and ill-fated relationship with Romeo [5].

Although Lord Capulet at first seems a responsible parent, by Act 3 scene 5 the audience are shown his rash and cruel side. His threat, 'hang! Beg! Starve! Die in the streets! / For by my soul I'll ne'er acknowledge thee', if Juliet will not marry Paris, links to the traditional expectation that a wealthy father would arrange his daughter's marriage. However, this causes Juliet to take the sleeping potion and therefore indirectly leads to her death [6].

Ultimately, the Montagues and the Capulets love their children and regret their actions, linking to the play's literary context of tragedy. Lady Montague dies of grief over Romeo's exile and, upon seeing Juliet's dead body, Lady Capulet says, 'O me! This sight of death is as a bell / That warns my old age to a sepulchre', suggesting she too is close to death [7]. Both fathers' inconsolable grief ends the family feud as they realise it is their own behaviour that has brought about the death of their children [8].

1. A clear introduction establishing the focus of the essay. AO1

2. A clear opening point, supported by a well-chosen quotation. Social context is successfully integrated. AO1/AO3

3. The first point is developed through further social context and interpretation of the effect of parent–child relationships. AO1/AO3

4. A new point expands the range of the essay and is supported by a well-chosen quotation and integrated social context. AO1/AO3

5. Social context is used to develop the paragraph and suggest the effects of parent–child relationships. AO1/AO3

6. The new point builds on the previous paragraph, using a well-chosen quotation and integrated social context. The effect of parent–child relationships is considered. AO1/AO3

7. The final paragraph expands the range of the essay further, integrating literary context and using a well-chosen quotation. AO1/AO3

8. The final sentence explores the effect of parent–child relationships and creates a brief conclusion. AO1

> ## Questions
>
> EXAM PRACTICE
> Spend 25 minutes writing an answer to Question 1b from page 58.
> Remember to use the plan you have already prepared.

Glossary

Abstract noun – a noun that is an idea or quality (such as: charity, compassion), rather than a concrete object.

Adjective – a word that describes a noun.

Adverb – a word that describes a verb.

Alliteration – a series of words beginning with the same sound or letter.

Analogy – a comparison used to explain or clarify an idea.

Atmosphere – the mood or emotion in a play.

Classical gods – deities mentioned in the myths and legends of ancient Greece and Rome.

Coincidence – different, unrelated events joining together by chance.

Double entendre – a word or phrase that can have two interpretations, one of which is rude.

Dramatic irony – when the audience of a play is aware of something that a character on stage isn't.

Duality – when something has two aspects or elements, often in contrast with each other.

Empathy – sympathising with someone else's circumstances or emotions.

Fate – the idea that the events in someone's life are outside their personal control and are predetermined by some higher power.

Foreboding – a feeling that something bad is going to happen.

Foreshadow – warn about or indicate a future event.

Guilt – regret for something you have done.

Homophone – a word with the same sound as another but a different meaning.

Honour – respect and esteem; doing what is morally right.

Hyperbole – exaggeration to emphasise an idea.

Imagery – words used to create a picture in the imagination.

Imperative – an order.

Innuendo – a phrase that contains an additional (usually rude or unkind) suggested meaning.

Irony – something that seems the opposite of what was expected; deliberately using words that mean the opposite of what is intended.

Juxtaposition – placing two contrasting things side by side.

Masquerade – a ball or party where the guests wear masks and costumes.

Melancholy – sad and thoughtful.

Metaphor – a descriptive technique, using comparison to say one thing is something else.

Modal verb – a verb that shows the necessity or possibility of another verb (such as: could eat, should eat, might eat).

Noun – an object or thing.

Noun phrase – a group of words making up a noun.

Omen – a sign of future events, good or bad.

Oxymoron – contradictory words placed together to create a phrase.

Parallel structure – using the same pattern of words in a sentence or phrase for effect.

Patriarchal – relating to a society ruled by men.

Pattern of three – three related ideas, placed together for emphasis.

Personification – writing about an object, place or idea as if it has human characteristics.

Pronoun – a word that takes the place of a noun (such as: I, she, them, it).

Pun – using a word that has a double meaning (the second meaning usually being rude) in order to create humour; a word can also be substituted for a similar sounding word with a rude meaning.

Regal – like, or appropriate for, royalty.

Repetition – saying a word or phrase more than once, for effect.

Rhetorical question – a question asked in order to create thought rather than to get a specific answer.

Sibilance – repetition of s sounds to create an effect.

Simile – a descriptive technique, using comparison to say one thing is 'like' or 'as' something else.

Sin – an immoral act.

Soliloquy – a speech given alone on stage (or that other characters present cannot hear) to reveal what a character is thinking.

Sonnet – a fourteen-line poem, usually with ten syllables per line and exploring the theme of love.

Stichomythia – when characters speak alternate lines of dialogue, each time repeating and developing a word or image from the previous speaker's line.

Symbolise – when an object or colour represents a specific idea or meaning.

Synaesthesia – describing one sense by using another.

Traditional – long-established or old-fashioned.

Tragedy – an event that causes great suffering; a play that explores tragic events.

Unrequited love – when love isn't returned.

Verb – a doing or action word.

Verb phrase – a group of words making up a verb.

Wordplay – using different meanings and ambiguities in words, often to create humour.

Answers

Pages 4–5

Quick Test

1. Sampson, one of the Capulet servants.
2. Benvolio wants to stop the fight but Tybalt is ready to join in.
3. He thinks she is too young to get married.
4. Romeo wants to see Rosaline but Benvolio hopes that Romeo will fall in love with someone else.

Exam Practice

Analysis might include the following: Sampson using wordplay to joke about taking the virginity of the Montague girls; Tybalt questioning Benvolio's commitment to peace and his use of repetition and pattern of three to emphasise his aggressive nature; Lord Montague's short exclamative phrases showing his aggression and eagerness to fight the Capulets, compared with his wife ordering him to calm down.

Pages 6–7

Quick Test

1. Lady Capulet is more romantic while the Nurse talks about physical aspects and makes sexual jokes.
2. They are masked because it is a masquerade.
3. He forgets about her as soon as he sees Juliet.
4. Because Tybalt disobeys him by wanting to fight Romeo.
5. A sonnet; this traditional form of love poetry emphasises the romance between them.

Exam Practice

Analysis might include the following: Lady Capulet's imperative makes marriage sound like a social necessity rather than something romantic; Romeo's metaphor implies love at first sight by suggesting Juliet shines more brightly than everything else in the room; the use of death imagery shows the pain Juliet will feel if she cannot be with Romeo.

Pages 8–9

Quick Test

1. To remind the audience that Romeo and Juliet's love is doomed.
2. She worries they are rushing things and describes her hope that their love will grow.
3. When she suggests that they get married.
4. He is surprised that Romeo has so quickly forgotten about Rosaline.

Exam Practice

Analysis might include the following: Juliet's rhetorical question and simile explore the family feud as an obstacle to her and Romeo's love; Romeo uses metaphor to explore how his family name is an obstacle; he also uses metaphor to describe the pain he would feel if she didn't return his love.

Pages 10–11

Quick Test

1. He is more happy and jovial.
2. That afternoon.
3. She wants news of Romeo and whether he will be true to his promise to marry her.
4. The Nurse and Friar Laurence.

Exam Practice

Analysis might include the following: Juliet's desperation to hear from Romeo is conveyed by her wish for his thoughts to reach her and wanting them to travel faster than light; Romeo uses personification of death to suggest that marrying Juliet is the only thing he wants in life – after that he doesn't care what happens (Shakespeare uses dramatic irony because the audience know he will die); images of speed and measurement are used by the Friar to encourage Romeo to be sensible.

Pages 12–13

Quick Test

1. Benvolio appears to want to avoid any confrontation whereas Mercutio is ready to create a fight with the Capulets.
2. He doesn't fully explain why he won't fight Tybalt; Mercutio thinks it is cowardice so fights Tybalt himself; Romeo holds Mercutio back, at which point he is stabbed by Tybalt.
3. At first, Juliet thinks Romeo has died.
4. Juliet is initially horrified that she is married to the killer of her cousin, but her love for Romeo is stronger than her horror and she reasons that Tybalt would have killed him.

Exam Practice

Analysis might include the following: how, as he dies, Mercutio curses the Montagues and Capulets for being the cause of his death; metaphor is used to convey Romeo being overcome by aggression; the repetition of 'blood' shows Lady Capulet wants vengeance for the death of Tybalt, but the use of rhyme emphasises how she sees it as justice.

Pages 14–15

Quick Test

1. Mantua.
2. In Act 1, he wanted Paris to wait another two years; in Act 3, he wants the marriage to take place in three days' time.
3. Lord Capulet is more sympathetic than Lady Capulet.
4. He threatens to disown her.

Exam Practice

Analysis might include the following: Romeo's use of hyperbole and pattern of three to describe the pain he feels at the idea of being separated from Juliet; the powerful abstract noun 'vengeance' shows Lady Capulet's desire for revenge, and her determination is emphasised by the modal verb 'will' and her confident statement 'fear thou not'; Lord Capulet's list of aggressive verbs show his anger, emphasised through the use of exclamation marks that suggest shouting, and by his threat never to speak to Juliet again.

Pages 16–17

Quick Test

1. Because he knows things that most of the other characters do not: Romeo and Juliet's marriage and the sleeping potion that Juliet has taken.
2. He plans to fake Juliet's death then contact Romeo so he can meet her at the tomb and take her back to Mantua.

3. After Juliet apologises to Lord Capulet, he brings the marriage forward by a day (meaning the Friar's letter won't reach Romeo in time).
4. A happy atmosphere as the marriage is prepared; a sad, distraught atmosphere as Juliet is found apparently dead and the wedding is changed to preparations for a funeral.

Exam Practice
Analysis might include the following: Juliet's abstract nouns to show her anxiety about taking the sleeping potion; Lady Capulet using metaphor to describe Juliet's importance to her, her repeated verbs that show her desperation for Juliet to be alive and her feeling that she will die from grief; personification of death and Lord Capulet's metaphor that his grief is so strong he cannot express it.

Pages 18–19
Quick Test
1. He dreams that he is dead and Juliet brings him back to life with a kiss. There is dramatic irony because we know he is going to die. The dream also foreshadows the actual death scene in which Juliet tries to kiss poison from his lips.
2. Friar Laurence's letters didn't reach Romeo.
3. Romeo drinks poison and Juliet stabs herself.
4. Their parents.
Exam Practice
Analysis might include the following: his exclamation uses the stars to represent fate, blaming them for Juliet's death; repeated images of rage show his passion and grief for Juliet as he threatens Balthasar not to disturb him; personification of death that shows his grief but is also used to emphasise the strength and wonder of Juliet's still–intact beauty.

Pages 20–21
Quick Test
1. The Capulets and the Montagues, Prince Escalus and Paris.
2. The Nurse and the servants.
3. He is the head of the household, people follow his orders and he decides who is allowed to court Juliet.
4. To improve status.
Exam Practice
Comments might include the following: Paris follows social expectations by asking Lord Capulet's permission to court Juliet; it is quite surprising that Lord Capulet emphasises the importance of Juliet's choice; his protectiveness may be explained by the reference to her being his only child and therefore his heir; it is clear that, in the time the play is set, thirteen is not an unusually early age to get married, although Capulet wants Paris to wait for two years.

Pages 22–23
Quick Test
1. It was popular with the English who thought it a very fashionable place and were interested in its reputation for passionate people and violent family rivalries.
2. The War of the Roses, the break from the Catholic Church and food/tax riots.
3. To make the audience, especially its rowdier members, laugh.
4. Mercutio's curse on the Montagues and the Capulets; the reason for Friar Laurence's letter never reaching Romeo.

Exam Practice
Comments might include the following: Sampson boasts about fighting with the Montagues and uses wordplay to joke that he will take the virginity of the Montague girls; the pair's use of stichomythia to create a fast, witty rhythm to their conversation; Sampson's double entendre where 'stand' can also mean erection, followed by his double entendre where 'pretty piece' can mean handsome or well-endowed, which Gregory continues with 'tool' meaning either sword or penis; the conversation ends with the possibility of violence.

Pages 24–25
Quick Test
1. The deaths of Mercutio, Tybalt, Paris, Romeo, Juliet and Lady Montague, as well as the different obstacles that are put in the way of Romeo and Juliet's love, such as Romeo's banishment.
2. Romeo and Juliet.
3. The balcony scene in Act 2 scene 2.
4. To appeal to his audience but also as a technique to heighten the tragic events of the play.
Exam Practice
Comments might include the following: Shakespeare creates dramatic irony as Juliet is unaware of the tragic events of the previous scene; her image of Romeo attaining a kind of immortality is also ironic as the audience know that his tragic death will come earlier than the two lovers expect; the reference to stars also implies how their destinies are already laid out for them; the exploration of death and fate continues with her reference to heaven; the dramatic irony also continues in her expectation that the Nurse has good news about Romeo.

Pages 26–27
Quick Test
1. Lord Montague describes Romeo's melancholy, solitary behaviour; it is due to his unrequited love for Rosaline.
2. He forgets Rosaline very quickly, making the audience wonder how genuine his love is for Juliet.
3. Imagery of nature, value and heavenliness/unearthliness.
4. Climbing the walls in the Capulet grounds despite the danger and agreeing to marry Juliet the next day.
Exam Practice
Analysis might include the following: Romeo's metaphor to suggest he is dead or that life isn't worth living without the love of Rosaline; his exclamation shows his certainty that no one is better than Rosaline and this is emphasised through hyperbole; personification of love, and possibly a reference to Cupid, conveys how love has filled him with happiness and also made him brave.

Pages 28–29
Quick Test
1. Because he has married Juliet who is Tybalt's cousin; he is now part of the family and does not want to worsen the feud.
2. Torture and death.
3. Personification of death.
4. No one.

Answers

Exam Practice

Analysis might include the following: the hyperbole shows his love for Juliet by conveying his agony at the idea of being separated from her; the personification of the tomb and his use of aggressive verbs shows his reckless desire to kill himself; metaphors convey his love for Juliet and his wish to die alongside her.

Pages 30–31

Quick Test

1. 13.
2. She doesn't talk much, allowing her mother and nurse to dominate, and she agrees to consider Paris as a potential husband.
3. She would give up her family.
4. They both use religious imagery and death imagery.

Exam Practice

Analysis might include the following: the repetition of Romeo's name emphasises her feelings for him, as well as highlighting her frustration at how his family is an obstacle, which is conveyed by the verbs 'refuse' and 'deny'; she is embarrassed at having been heard but uses the noun phrase 'true-love passion' to make her feelings clear; the use of 'foot' symbolises her willingness to obey her husband, matching the social expectations of the time, and this is emphasised by the submissive verbs 'lay' and 'follow'.

Pages 32–33

Quick Test

1. To have him killed by poison.
2. The Nurse suggests she forgets Romeo and marries Paris.
3. Stay faithful to Romeo.
4. She tries to kiss the poison that he has used from his lips.

Exam Practice

Analysis might include the following: her exclamations and oxymorons show frustration and confusion, suggesting her inner turmoil at finding that her beloved husband has killed her cousin; the metaphor is used to threaten her suicide; the personification of the dagger tragically shows that she sees death as her only relief and this is emphasised by the verb phrase 'let me die'.

Pages 34–35

Quick Test

1. A word that has a double meaning (the second meaning often being rude) to create humour, or a word substituted for a similar-sounding word to add a rude meaning.
2. Sex and the penis.
3. He physically restrains him from fighting, which allows Tybalt to stab him.
4. It is still full of humorous puns but they are all linked to death rather than sex.

Exam Practice

Analysis might include the following: his rude humour, describing Rosaline's body from her foot to her vagina and suggesting she's ready for sex; the adjective 'saucy' suggesting he is rude and cheeky, which is emphasised by the noun 'ropery'; the plural **pronoun** blaming the Montagues and the Capulets as he acknowledges his imminent death.

Pages 36–37

Quick Test

1. Peace and the Montagues.
2. Villain.
3. His courtesy and honesty.

Exam Practice

Analysis might include the following: how he thinks Romeo is so bad that it wouldn't be a 'sin' to kill him; the noun 'villain' suggests Romeo is dishonourable, has low status and is worthless; this idea appears again in the word 'consort' (which he also used to demean Mercutio) and 'wretched', and he uses 'boy' to belittle Romeo.

Pages 38–39

Quick Test

1. It could be because of Prince Escalus's ultimatum or it could be that he is trying to make a good impression on his potential son-in-law.
2. Other girls of her age are married, and so was Lady Capulet when she was Juliet's age.
3. He suddenly decides that Juliet isn't too young to be married and that the wedding should be in three days' time.

Exam Practice

Analysis might include the following: Lord Capulet's speech uses parallel structure to show he is protective of Juliet and worries about her marrying too young; Lady Capulet's imperative verbs show her encouraging Juliet to marry but the metaphors imply that she thinks it will make Juliet happy; the cruel metaphor shows her anger and inability to understand Juliet; the simile conveys Capulet's love of his daughter, accompanied by grief at her apparent early death.

Pages 40–41

Quick Test

1. She prevaricates, rather than instantly passing on Romeo's message.
2. Her own daughter, who would be Juliet's age, is dead.
3. She warns him not to hurt Juliet.
4. The Nurse and Lady Capulet.

Exam Practice

Analysis might include the following: the imperative and the repetition of the adjective 'happy' show she is excited and eager for Juliet to fall in love; her metaphor 'fool's paradise', the adjective 'gross' and the reference to youth show she is protective of Juliet; the comparisons and adjectives show that she wants what is best for Juliet and hopes to convince her to marry Paris, however, this also shows that she doesn't know Juliet as well as she thought.

Pages 42–43

Quick Test

1. Tybalt.
2. Because he is a relation and a friend of Romeo.
3. To take one's time: 'Wisely and slow; they stumble that run fast'.
4. She is threatening to kill herself and there seems no other way to keep her from marrying Paris.

Analysis might include the following: Benvolio uses contrasting bird imagery to suggest that Romeo will find someone more attractive than Rosaline at the Capulet feast; parallel structure is used to encourage Romeo not to be too consumed by his passions, as this recklessness could lead to his downfall; the Friar uses a rhetorical question to encourage Romeo to reconsider suicide, using metaphor to suggest that he would be killing Juliet at the same time, and adding the adjective 'damned' to remind him that suicide is a sin.

Pages 44–45

Quick Test
1. A saint or a holy figure.
2. A pilgrim or worshipper.
3. Romeo's words suggest they will achieve everlasting love through death.
4. It is written as a sonnet, a traditional and intensely romantic form of love poetry.

Exam Practice
Analysis might include the following: the religious imagery suggests that Romeo worships Juliet and that his love is pure; the two comparisons link love to gentleness, as well as drawing on the senses via **synaesthesia** to create an intimate, sensual mood; the oxymoron conveys the pleasure of being in love and the pain of not being constantly with the one you love.

Pages 46–47

Quick Test
1. Stichomythia.
2. Mercutio's death is accidently caused by Romeo trying to stop the fight; Paris attacks Romeo because he thinks he has come to dishonour the Capulet tomb.
3. Regret.
4. Juliet, Tybalt, and – to some extent in Act 3 scene 5 – Lady Capulet.

Exam Practice
Analysis might include the following: the simile presents fighting as reckless and dangerous; violence is used as a threat to make Juliet obey her father, shown in the contrast between the submissive verb 'go' and the more aggressive alternative 'drag'; Romeo tries to avoid conflict but the abstract noun 'fury' shows he cannot control his anger.

Pages 48–49

Quick Test
1. The fight between the Montagues and Capulets at the start of the play.
2. That Romeo has killed himself, and that Romeo and Tybalt are both dead.
3. That it's better than death.
4. Committing suicide by stabbing themselves.

Exam Practice
Analysis might include the following: Romeo's metaphors show how confusing he finds unrequited love and the sorrow it has caused him; Juliet's metaphors and contrasts show her shock at discovering that the man she loves has killed her cousin, and this is emphasised by the use of rhetorical question and exclamation; the pattern of three emphasises Juliet's anguish at having to marry Paris.

Pages 50–51

Quick Test
1. Lord Capulet.

2. Boys appear to have more freedom while girls stay at home and have life decisions made for them by their parents.
3. She dies of grief after Romeo is exiled.
4. They set a bad example by continuing the feud; Lord Capulet behaves in an aggressive manner while Lady Capulet pushes her daughter to get married.

Exam Practice
Analysis might include the following: the adjectives show Lord Montague's anxiety about his son's behaviour and this is emphasised by the repetition of the intensifier 'so'; the adverb 'happily' and the adjective 'joyful' show Lady Capulet's wish for Juliet to be happy, but also her lack of understanding of her daughter and her carelessness in wanting her married when she is still so young; the contrasting religious language shows how Lord Capulet's love for Juliet turns to rage when she disobeys him.

Pages 52–53

Quick Test
1. To emphasise, from the start, the theme of fate and the idea that our lives are predetermined.
2. He believes they are manipulating him for their amusement.
3. Juliet takes the sleeping potion and calls his name, just as Romeo says 'Here's to my love' before poisoning himself.
4. He imagines he is dead and Juliet comes to wake him.

Exam Practice
Analysis might include the following: Juliet appears to have an omen of Romeo's death, using a simile to describe how he looks like a corpse in a tomb; Romeo uses personification, blaming the stars for Juliet's death as if they represent some higher power; personification is used again to express Romeo's belief that he has been unlucky and this was always how the story of his life would end.

Pages 54–55

Quick Test
1. Four days.
2. Mercutio, Tybalt, Paris, Romeo, Juliet and Lady Montague.
3. The Friar's letter misses Romeo; Juliet wakes just after Romeo kills himself.
4. Fate.

Exam Practice
Analysis might include the following: Romeo's sense of foreboding before he goes to the Capulet feast is shown through words like 'fearful' and 'vile forfeit', while the stars are used to symbolise fate and his belief that he is being led to an 'untimely death'; the Friar personifies time and blames it for the tragic events that have unfolded in the tomb; the Friar explains the chain of events that led to Romeo and Juliet's suicide, linking it partly to Tybalt's 'untimely' death and Romeo's subsequent banishment.

Pages 58–61

Possible Questions
Use the mark scheme on page 80 to self-assess your strengths and weaknesses. The estimated grade boundaries are included so you can assess your progress towards your target grade.

Answers

Quick Test

1. AO2. Analysis of Shakespeare's language, structure and form. All ideas should be related to a specific quotation from the extract.
2. AO1 and AO3. Clear understanding of ideas in the play; a well-structured and clearly expressed response; quotations included as evidence. Link explanations to the play's context and consider how it affects meaning.
3. Planning focusses your thoughts and allows you to produce a well-structured essay.

Exam Practice

Ideas for Part A might include the following: Romeo's worshipful language, combined with his suggestive language; Juliet's mirroring of this religious and flirtatious speech; the effect of their opening speech up to the kiss being written as a sonnet; the family problem that is established in their relationship.

Ideas for Part B might include the following: Romeo's feelings of unrequited love for Rosaline; the possibility that his love for Juliet is as temporary as his love for Rosaline; secrecy and rash decisions due to love; the Friar's hope that love can resolve the family rivalry; Romeo and Juliet's inability to live without each other.

Pages 70–73

Exam Practice

Use the mark scheme below to self-assess your strengths and weaknesses. Work up from the bottom, putting a tick by things you have fully accomplished, a ½ by skills that are in place but need securing, and underlining areas that need particular development. The estimated grade boundaries are included so you can assess your progress towards your target grade.

| Grade | Part A | Part B | |
	AO2 (20 marks)	AO1 (15 marks)	AO3 (5 marks)
6–7+	Analysis of the full range of Shakespeare's methods. Thorough exploration of the effects of these methods. Accurate range of subject terminology.	A convincing, well-structured essay that answers the question fully. Clear interpretation of a range of different aspects of the play. Quotations and references are well-chosen and integrated into sentences. The response covers the whole play.	Exploration is linked to specific aspects of the play's contexts to show a detailed understanding. Context is integrated with interpretation.
4–5	Explanation of Shakespeare's different methods. Clear understanding of the effects of these methods. Accurate use of subject terminology.	A clear essay that always focusses on the exam question. Some interpretation of different aspects of the play. Quotations and references support ideas effectively. The response refers to different points in the play.	References to relevant aspects of context show a clear understanding.
2–3	Identification of some different methods used by Shakespeare to convey meaning. Some subject terminology.	The essay has some good ideas that are mostly relevant. There is an attempt to interpret a few aspects of the play. Some quotations and references are used to support the ideas.	Some awareness of how ideas in the play link to its context.